About this Learning Guide

Shmoop Will Make You a Better Lover*
*of Literature, History, Poetry, Life...

Our lively learning guides are written by experts and educators who want to show your brain a good time. Shmoop writers come primarily from Ph.D. programs at top universities, including Stanford, Harvard, and UC Berkeley.

Want more Shmoop? We cover literature, poetry, bestsellers, music, US history, civics, biographies (and the list keeps growing). Drop by our website to see the latest.

www.shmoop.com

Table of Contents

Introduction

In a Nutshell

The Lovely Bones (2002) is American author Alice Sebold's first novel. The story is narrated by Susie Salmon, a fourteen-year-old girl who has been raped and killed by her serial killer neighbor in suburban Pennsylvania. That's right, Susie is telling her story from the afterlife. She weaves back and forth in time from the date of her death in 1973, remembering her life, peering into the mind of her killer, and watching the love ones she left behind. It's a gruesome and horrifying story, but also one of hope and renewal.

The Lovely Bones has sold millions of copies and is totally at home on the bestseller lists. A book buying frenzy ensued after Pulitzer Prize winning author Ana Quindlen announced on *The Today Show* that *The Lovely Bones* was *the* must read book of summer 2002. Critics loved it, for the most part, and it's won A Bram Stoker Award, among others. Peter Jackson, of *Lord of the Rings* fame, even directed the 2009 film adaptation. Critics didn't really like the film (it got a rotten tomato), complaining it's not dark enough and that the afterlife depicted is too fluffy. But Stanley Tucci was nominated for an Oscar for his terrifying portrayal of Susie's killer. And whether or not you agree with the movie's version of the afterlife, the film does a nice job of giving us some of the visuals that make the story so chilling and beautiful, and providing us with the mood and feel of the 1970s.

Sebold began writing *The Lovely Bones* around 1996 when she was 33, but had to put it down to write about a tragic event from her past – being raped by a stranger when she was eighteen. She says,

[…] after writing the first chapter of Lovely Bones, in which Susie is raped and killed, there was some urging on Susie's part that I get my own business out of the way before writing further into her story. When I say "on Susie's part" I mean: the demands of her wanting to tell her story and using me to do so meant that I had to unload my story someplace else. It wasn't going to fit into the book I wanted to write for her. (source)

Sounds like Susie is a pretty bossy ghost. The result is Sebold's debut book, *Lucky* (1999), a well received piece of non-fiction about the rape and the aftermath, including Sebold testifying against her rapist in court, which sent him to prison. You can read part of *Lucky* here, on Google Books.

Sebold studied with some literary legends, including Raymond Carver and Tess Gallagher. She lives in California with her husband, the novelist Glen David Gold, who says, "People who find living with a writer romantic often can't work with the reality. But Alice and I have complementary neuroses. If I look grumpy, she says, 'Is it the adverbs, dear?'" (source). Of

her dreams and goals, Sebold says, "I just want to write and read and walk my dog. You know, I'm very simple" (source).

Why Should I Care?

Why is *The Lovely Bones* so popular? One obvious reason is that it's a book about a serial killer. Serial killers (a term coined in the 1960s) are everywhere in American pop culture. There's Dexter, Norman Bates (from *Psycho*), and Hannibal Lecter (ever since *The Silence of the Lambs* Anthony Hopkins gives us the shivers), to name just a few. Serial killers pop up in our art, music, movies, soap operas, and books. There seems to be an insatiable appetite for serial killer fiction.

But *The Lovely Bones* is pretty different from your average serial killer thriller. Though the story is definitely dark and spine-tingling at times, the focus is really on the victim, Susie Salmon, and not the killer, Mr. Harvey. When author Alice Sebold was "[g]rowing up in the Philadelphia suburbs [she] was haunted by news stories about murdered girls." She remembers that "their story wasn't in the newspaper; it was always the story of the murderer. The girls seemed almost disposable" (source).

Though Susie Salmon tries to understand her killer, he is not the main focus of the book. The women and girls he hurts, and the incredibly difficult process the Salmon family undergoes to heal, take center stage.

So, what do you think? What accounts for the huge popularity of *The Lovely Bones*? Does it live up to the reviews? Will it stand the test of time? Should it be taught in schools?

Book Summary

Meet our narrator, Susie "like the fish" Salmon (1.1). She's been dead since December 16, 1973. She was fourteen years old when she was raped and murdered by her neighbor. Here's how it happened. It's a cold snowy afternoon. After school, Susie takes a shortcut through the cornfield to her suburban Pennsylvania home. Mr. Harvey (who she recognizes but doesn't know) is in the cornfield. He's built an underground shelter, with a door that's covered with earth. He piques Susie's curiosity and lures her into the hole. She quickly learns this is a mistake, and he rapes and then kills her. Right now she's in heaven, which she soon learns is her personal heaven – everybody gets one when they die.

On December 9, the detective in charge of Susie's case, Len Fenerman, calls Susie's mom and dad, Abigail and Jack Salmon, and tells them they've found Susie's elbow bone. From her heaven, Susie watches her parents in bed, unable to talk. It begins to storm. The next morning, Jack breaks the news of the elbow bone to his other daughter, Lindsey, who's thirteen. She throws up. Later that day the police try digging up the cornfield, even though the snow and rain have screwed up their crime scene.

Susie's schoolbooks and class notes are found, including a love letter from Ray Singh, Susie's first and only love. He'd slipped it into her books the day before she died. She didn't get to read it when she was alive. Ray has a perfect alibi, but the rumors wreak havoc on his school life. Susie watches with frustration as her murderer, Mr. Harvey, who builds dollhouses for a living, calmly goes on with his life. On December 15th, Len Fenerman tells the Salmons that Susie is probably dead.

We jump around a bit in time. When Susie leaves Earth, she touches Ruth Connors, a school friend, and Ruth becomes obsessed with her. Mr. Harvey collapses the underground room where he raped and killed Susie. Then he puts her "body parts" (4.1) in a bag, which he puts in his garage, while he goes up for a shower. Susie will learn later that he killed other girls before her. In the shower, Mr. Harvey thinks about how nice it was to kill Susie. Mr. Harvey puts the bag with Susie's body parts into a safe and dumps the safe into a sinkhole about eight miles from their Pennsylvania neighborhood.

On December 23, Susie's dad smashes some miniature ships a the bottle, which Susie often helped him with. He sees Susie's projected reflection in each piece of glass. Afterwards, Susie's four-year-old brother Buckley finds his dad and comforts him. Meanwhile, Mr. Harvey gets the idea to build a tent-like structure. After Jack Salmon breaks the ships in bottles, he happens to walk to Mr. Harvey's back yard and finds him making this odd structure.

Jack Salmon helps Mr. Harvey assemble the structure and talks to him. Susie is trying to send her dad ghostly messages, and she must have succeed because Jack begins to suspect Mr. Harvey of Susie's murder. He calls Detective Len Fenerman with his suspicions. Len Fenerman investigates. He thinks Harvey is weird, but doesn't find any evidence to make him a suspect. On Christmas day Samuel Heckler comes to visit Lindsey, beginning their romance. Meanwhile, Jack tries to teach Buckley how to play Monopoly and explain to him that his sister is dead.

Susie remembers hanging out with Ray for the first time, and meeting Ruth, after Ruth is harassed by teachers because of her realistic drawings of nude women. These things happened two weeks before she died. After Susie's death, Ruth spends lots of time in the cornfield in the early mornings. One day she meets Ray there, and they become friends.

Susie keeps a close eye on her killer. She learns that Mr. Harvey has dreams of killing women and children. She learns that he moved around a lot as a child, that his dad build strange buildings from scavenged material, and that his dad abandoned his mother on the side of the

road when Harvey was a child.

Susie's funeral service takes place two months after her death. Susie's grandmother (Abigail Salmon's mom) Lynn has flown in for the service. Mr. Harvey shows up to the funeral. Lynn and Lindsey don't recognize who he is, but they realize he's Susie's killer.

In the summer of 1974, Susie watches as Lindsey and Samuel begin a sexual relationship at the Gifted and Talented Symposium. Susie also learns that Ruth desires women in a sexual way, and that Ruth has become devoted to writing poetry about Susie.

Meanwhile, there's no progress on Susie's case. Jack Salmon is convinced of Mr. Harvey's guilt, and he calls the police constantly. Eventually, Len Fenerman tells him to stop, because there's no evidence to accuse Harvey. That night, Jack sees a light in the cornfield from his window. He goes out there with his baseball bat and almost attacks Susie's friend Clarissa, who's out there waiting for her boyfriend Brian Nelson. In an attempt to protect his girlfriend, Brian takes the baseball bat and beats Jack with it, landing him at the hospital. At the hospital, Abigail Salmon runs into Len Fenerman and they begin an affair.

That fall, Lindsey gets the idea from her dad that she should break into Mr. Harvey's house and find evidence to connect him with Susie's murder. Around Thanksgiving, she does it. When Lindsey is in Harvey's house, Susie learns about Harvey's other victims. Meanwhile Lindsey finds the evidence she needs and escapes just before Harvey catches her.

That afternoon, while some other policeman are interviewing Mr. Harvey about Lindsey's break-in, Len Fenerman is continuing his affair with Abigail Salmon at the mall. As they begin to make love, Mr. Harvey packs up and flees town. The following summer, Abigail leaves home and family. She spends some time in her father's cabin and then moves to California and takes a job at a winery.

In the fall, Grandma Lynn calls Jack and says she's moving in. That December, Mr. Harvey has been gone over a year, and nobody has been able to find him. Susie feels sorry for Len Fenerman because he didn't solve the crime in time or get the lady. (Apparently, when Abigail left for California, she cut all ties to Len.) Len feels extremely guilty for not solving Susie's case.

Ray, Susie's crush, gets handsomer and handsomer as the years go by, and he leaves for college. Ruth moves to New York City and when she's not working, she roams the streets. When she sees a place where a dead girl was killed, she can see what happened. In December 1988, Len Fenerman learns that Susie's charm was found near the body of murdered girl found in 1976. Susie's dog Holiday dies and comes to Susie's heaven.

When Lindsey is 21, she and Samuel are riding a motorcycle back from her graduation. They have matching spiky haircuts. About eight miles from their turn-off, it's raining so hard they have to pull off the road. They find an abandoned Victorian house in the distance. Inside, they

make love and get engaged. They decide to buy the house and live in it. Then they run home in the rain to Jack, half naked.

Shortly after, in New York, Ruth learns that the sinkhole, where she correctly suspects Mr. Harvey buried Susie's body, is to be filled in. So, she makes plans to return to the Philadelphia suburb.

At the Salmon residence, Buckley tells his dad he wants more attention, and begs his dad to focus on him instead of Susie. Jack has a heart attack and is rushed to the hospital. Abigail hears about it and finally comes back to her family. She and Jack fall back in love in Jack's hospital room.

Meanwhile, Mr. Harvey is headed back to the old neighborhood, haunted by dreams of Lindsey Salmon escaping his clutches before. Ruth and Ray are reunited, and they drive out to the sinkhole. The same day, Mr. Harvey makes it to the neighborhood, but a suspicious cop makes him leave. He passes the sinkhole when Ruth is standing near the road, next to the car she and Ray are driving. When she sees Mr. Harvey's car, she sees all the women he killed. She passes out.

At that moment Susie falls from heaven and borrows Ruth's body. She gets Ray to take her across the way to Hal Heckler's empty bike shop and they make love. While Susie is in Ruth's body, Ruth hangs out in heaven with the dead girls she's been memorializing. Then she and Susie switch back. Also on that day, Jack Salmon is released from the hospital and there is a poignant family reunion back at the Salmon house.

As the novel comes to a close, we learn that Susie has moved on up to "wide wide heaven" and has made peace with her newfound existence. She gives us a final glimpse of Mr. Harvey. He's about to attempt another attack, but is foiled by a falling icicle. He plunges to his death into a ravine. Then Susie shows us Lindsey, Samuel, and their new baby, Abigail Suzanne, and that's the end of the story.

Prologue

- The narrator tells us about the snow globe on her father's desk. Inside the snow globe: a lone penguin.
- She remembers telling her father that she's afraid the penguin is lonely.
- She remembers her father's response, "Don't worry Susie, he has a nice life. He's trapped in a perfect world" (Prologue.1).

Chapter 1

- Meet our narrator, Susie "like the fish" Salmon (1.1). She's been dead since December 16, 1973. She was fourteen years old when she was murdered by her neighbor, Mr. Harvey.
- Here's what happened:
- It's snowing and Susie takes a shortcut, through the cornfield, to get home after school. She gets a little scared when she comes upon Mr. Harvey there in the dark.
- He makes small talk with her, and she says she has to go home.
- But then Mr. Harvey says he wants to show her this really cool "hiding place" (1.24) he built underground. It has a wooden hatch, covered with dirt. The hatch keeps it from caving in.
- Susie is a really curious girl, very interested in science and engineering.
- She feels the excitement of a young child making a new discovery. She's never been in any real danger, and she doesn't know enough to be afraid.
- So, she goes into the underground room with Mr. Harvey, marveling that he has dug out all that dirt. He's even dug shelves. A little battery operated lamp sheds light on the amazing structure.
- She thinks Harvey's weird, but like her dad said, he's "just a character" (1.42).
- Susie wants to know everything about the dirt room – how he built it, how he learned to build it.
- But Susie's "in transit" (1.44) between Earth and her heaven when Harvey takes it apart after her murder. She doesn't see him collapse the hole and put her body in a bag.
- She's in heaven now, and she can watch Earth.
- The hole is all closed up three days later, when the neighbor's dog finds her elbow with a little piece of cornhusk on it,.
- But back to the story of her murder:
- Next Harvey pressures Susie stay and have a coke, and starts asking her personal questions, like: Does she have a boyfriend? Is she a virgin?
- Now Susie *is* scared and tries to leave but Mr. Harvey tells her she isn't going anywhere.
- She fights as best she can, not having any knowledge of self defense, but loses.
- When he's kissing her, she thinks of her first and only other kiss, with Ray, a boy she has a crush on.
- She begs him not to, but Harvey brutally rapes her, stuffing the jingly pompom of her hat into her mouth when she screams.
- After, he shows her a knife and asks her if she loves him. She says yes, but he still kills her.

Chapter 2

- When Susie gets to heaven she thinks that everybody in heaven is surrounded by high schools like she is. She soon learns that this is her personal heaven, just like all the other

people up there.

- The people she sees in her heaven have desires that overlap with hers, making their heavens similar.
- Susie and her future roommate Holly meet on their fourth day in heaven.
- Neither one of them like heaven, but they realize that they've "been given [...] their simplest dreams" (2.17), like school, but no teachers and magazines for textbooks.
- A woman named Franny is Susie's "intake counselor" (2.19) becomes a mommy figure to them, because, naturally, they miss their mommies.
- On the fifth day, Susie and Holly are bored.
- Franny gives them Kool-Aid, and tells them the secret to life in heaven, "All you have to do is desire it, and understand why [...] it will come" (2.25). So, their heavens get bigger.
- December 9: Detective Fenerman calls Susie's mom and dad and tells him they've found Susie's elbow. Susie watches her parents in bed afterwards, unable to talk. It begins to storm.
- The next morning, Mr. Salmon breaks the news of the elbow to his other daughter, Lindsey, who's thirteen, and extremely gifted and talented. After she hears the news, she throws up.
- Later that day the police search try digging up the cornfield, even though the snow/rain, etc. screwed up their crime scene.
- They do find a copy of _To Kill A Mockingbird_ and establish that it's Susie's.
- On the 12th they find her notes from school, including a love letter from Ray Singh. Ray has a perfect alibi, but the rumors wreak havoc on his school life.
- Susie watches with frustration as Mr. Harvey calmly goes on with his life. She takes comfort in watching the family dog, Holiday.
- On the 15th, Fenerman tells the Salmon's that they think Susie's dead. The lab results are in. The dirt from the cornfield is full of blood.
- Susie's mom doesn't believe she's dead until Fenerman shows her Susie's jingly pompom hat, and tells her it was used to gag Susie. Meanwhile Susie fills her heaven with dogs for comfort.

Chapter 3

- When Susie flees from Earth, she touches Ruth Connors, a school friend.
- Ruth has a dream about it and tells her mom, but her mom thinks it's silly.
- Ruth looks at Susie's yearbook pictures.
- One days she sees Susie's friend Clarissa flirting and smooching with Brian Nelson in the hall.
- Then, Ruth breaks into Clarissa's locker and steals a scrapbook with pictures of Susie in it.
- Susie watches her mom from heaven, and remembers taking a picture of her mom, which showed a secret side of Abigail, which nobody had ever seen.

- Susie watches from heaven as her sister wakes up in the night and begins looking at Susie's stuff. She watches her find the picture of their mom's secret.
- On December 23, Susie watches as her dad thinks of her while looking at his collection of ships in bottles, many of which Susie helped him with. She watches him smash them up with a baseball bat, and he sees Susie's projected reflection in each piece of glass.
- Then he goes into Susie's room and starts crying on her bed. Her little brother Buckley finds him and comforts him.
- Susie's dad gets very confused, blurring Buckley and Susie in his mind for a few moments.

Chapter 4

- After Mr. Harvey kills Susie he collapses the hole and puts her "body parts" (4.1) in a bag, which he puts in the garage, while he goes up for a shower.
- Her blood leaks out, leaving a permanent stain, while he showers.
- Susie will learn later that he killed other girls before her. In the shower, he thinks about how nice it was to kill her.
- (Wait, we thought she was "in transit" (1.44) and couldn't see this part of the story?)
- In any case, Mr. Harvey puts the bag with Susie's body parts into a safe and dumps the safe into a sinkhole about eight miles from the Pennsylvania neighborhood.
- Afterwards, he walks around an industrial park.
- He finds Susie's charm bracelet in his pocket, and doesn't remember taking it off of her, or putting it in there.
- He removes the Pennsylvania keystone charm (Pennsylvania is "the keystone state") and throws the rest of it into a manmade lake.
- On December 23, Mr. Harvey gets the idea to build a new trap, this one out of cloth.
- After Mr. Salmon breaks the ships in bottles, he happens to walk to Mr. Harvey's back yard and finds him making it. He asks him about it and Harvey says it's a tent.
- Mr. Harvey tells him, "I'm sorry for your loss" (4.41).
- Susie's dad stays and helps him build the tent. At one point, Mr. Harvey goes upstairs to look at the bloody knife he used on Susie. This makes him think of the tent as a bridal tent.
- It starts snowing, and Mr. Salmon begs Susie to communicate with him.
- Suddenly, Susie's dad suspects Mr. Harvey. When Harvey comes out of the house with a stack of white sheets Mr. Salmon asks him what they are for.
- Mr. Harvey says they are "tarps." Mr. Salmon accuses him of having information about Susie's death. Mr. Harvey denies it, and Mr. Salmon helps him with the tarps.
- Mr. Salmon accuses Mr. Harvey again, but Mr. Harvey tells him to go away.

Chapter 5

- For a minute, Susie wishes her dad would go kill Mr. Harvey. She can feel her father's intense guilt over not having protected her.
- She watches him try to comfort Lindsey, but Lindsey doesn't want his help. She watches him call Detective Fenerman and tell him he thinks Harvey knows something.
- Fenerman goes to Harvey's and finds him odd, but not suspicious.
- Harvey is at work building dollhouses (that's how he makes his living). When Fenerman asks about the tent, Harvey says he builds it for his late wife Leah, every year, usually inside.
- Fenerman feels bad for him. Harvey tells Fenerman to talk to "the Ellis boy" (5.60) who has been accused of hurting neighborhood animals.
- When Fenerman calls Mr. Salmon, to tell him about it, Mr. Salmon says he heard that Mr. Harvey's wife was named Sophie. But Fenerman is sure Mr. Harvey said "Leah."
- Mr. Salmon writes both names in his notebook, unwittingly starting "a list of the dead" (5.81).
- On Christmas, Mr. Salmon and Lindsay are playing Monopoly when a boy, Samuel Heckler, comes to visit Lindsey.
- Mr. Salmon begins teaching Buckley the rules of Monopoly. He also tells him that Susie is dead, though Buckley doesn't really understand. He gives him Susie's Monopoly shoes, and Buckley keeps it on his dresser until it mysteriously disappears.
- Meanwhile, Lindsey and Samuel are in the kitchen and Samuel gives Lindsey a present – half of a gold heart. The other half is on a cord around his neck. Then Lindsey kisses him.

Chapter 6

- Two weeks before her murder, Susie gets to school a little bit late, and she's sneaking around behind the stage to avoid getting caught by the hall monitor. Suddenly, she hears Ray Singh – gorgeous, from India – tell her she's beautiful.
- He's up on the scaffold, skipping class, and he talks her into joining him. Just when they are about to kiss, they hear some teachers come onto the stage. They hear them talking with Ruth Connors.
- She's in trouble for drawing a realistic nude for art class. Someone had made a copy of it and passed it around. Susie and Ray had seen it, and it was really good. Ruth tries to defend her right to draw realistically.
- After the teachers finish hassling her, they leave. Ruth starts crying. Susie comes down to comfort her.
- Ruth shows Susie her amazing sketches, and they become friends.
- After Susie's death, Ruth spends lots of time in the cornfield, in the early mornings. One day she meets Ray there, and they become friends.
- One day, Susie watches from heaven as her dad goes to Ray's and meets his mom

Ruana.

- He tells Ruana he knows Ray didn't have anything to do with it, he just wants to talk to him.
- He tells her he suspects George Harvey. Ruana says that if she were him, she'd find the evidence and then kill him.
- Meanwhile, Detective Fenerman is waiting for Jack Salmon, Susie's dad, with Susie's mom, Abigail.
- He tells her he thinks they'll catch Susie's killer. He also tells her she reminds him of his late wife. Soon, Jack Salmon arrives; she and the detective begin to talk to him.

Chapter 7

- Susie watches as Buckley, his friend Nate, and Holiday the dog run up the stairs.
- Buckley tells Nate he can see Susie, and that Susie talks to him and kisses his cheek.
- Buckley takes Nate into her room. After her death, Holiday finds Susie's stash of private stuff, and has strewn the items around the room.
- Now Buckley finds a bloody twig she'd saved two years before.
- (Flashback)
- Susie is babysitting Buckley. He gets a twig stuck in his throat and starts chocking.
- She'd grabbed the keys to her dad's Mustang and drives him to the hospital, saving his life.
- She saves the twig as a memento.
- Her Grandma Lynn says she will live long as a result of her heroics.
- But Grandma Lynn wasn't right at all.
- In heaven, Susie sees a line of crows, holding twigs in their beaks. When she leaves the gazebo (where she watches Earth) to go back to her and Holly's duplex, the crows follow.
- She wonders if Buckley can really see her.

Chapter 8

- Susie can see Mr. Harvey's dreams. She watches him "dream [...] of buildings for about ninety days" (8.1).
- His favorite building dream is of the Church of the Transfiguration, in the Vologda region of Russia.
- He dreamed it that night, after he killed Susie, and keeps dreaming it until the other dreams – dreams of women and kids – come back to him.
- These dreams are the "*not still* dreams" (8.2).
- Susie can see Mr. Harvey's memories of being a kid with his mother, and his father.
- Young Harvey tells people his dad is "a builder." He couldn't tell them the truth – that his

father "worked in the desert, and [...] built shacks out of broken glass and old wood" (8.3).
- His father taught him about building.
- When Harvey dreams the *not still* dreams he looks at his dad's old sketchbooks, trying to be satisfied with the work he does (building dollhouses).
- But then he'll start dreaming of his mother, of the day his father abandoned her on the road in Truth or Consequences, New Mexico, the last day Mr. Harvey saw her.

Chapter 9

- Susie's memorial service is tomorrow, two months after her death. Her Grandma Lynn, Abigail's mother, arrives tonight via limo from the airport. She's drinking champagne and wearing her mink coat.
- Upon arrival, she calls for "stiff drinks" (9.5). Lindsey creeps away to hide, but Buckley is overjoyed.
- Lynn is very concerned with fashion, thinness, and drinking.
- Before the murder, she was considered the ultimate bad influence, but now she's a force pulling the numb family out of depression.
- Right away she gives Abigail a makeover, and then teaches Lindsey to put on makeup.
- Lindsey sleeps in her makeup so she can wear it to the memorial. When she wakes up, she goes to Susie's room to find something to wear.
- Grandma Lynn comes in and finds her a dress, which happens to belong to Clarissa, and helps Lindsey with her makeup.
- Samuel, his brother Hal, Len Fenerman, Clarissa and Brian, and Ruth are at the funeral.
- Clarissa recognizes her dress on Lindsey, but doesn't say anything.
- Ray Singh doesn't attend. He stays home looking at the studio shot Susie gave him before she died. He doesn't want to trap Susie by mooning over her picture, but doesn't want to destroy it.
- So, he puts it in a book of Indian poetry, where he and his mom press flowers.
- Near the end of the service Lynn looks over at the church door and sees a man standing behind Detective Fenerman. She points, saying, "By the door, that's him."
- Lindsey looks at the man Lynn's pointing at. They make eye contact, and Lindsey feels a surge of recognition. Then she passes out.
- While everybody gathers around her, George Harvey walks away.

Chapter 10

- It's summer now, and Lindsey, Samuel, and Ruth are attending "the statewide Gifted and Talented Symposium" (10.1).
- Samuel worships his brother Hal, who runs a bike shop behind the railroad tracks across

from the sinkhole, and lives at home in an apartment on top of the garage.

- Ruth is becoming more devoted to her Susie poetry and has become a vegetarian since Susie died.
- Lindsey draws a fish on her nametag – when people see her name, they think of Susie, bloody and butchered. Ruth asks her about it in the cafeteria one day.
- Susie watches Ruth write and dream about her more and more.
- She discovers that Ruth has sexual desires for women.
- Susie learns she doesn't have to stay in the gazebo to watch Earth; she can walk heaven's fields and still see.
- One day, she asks Franny if there's another heaven, where her ancestors are, where nobody can remember their time on Earth.
- Franny says there is, but to go there, you have to stop worrying about Earth. Susie can't imagine getting to that point.
- That night, Ruth comes to Lindsey's bed after dreaming of Susie. She confides in Lindsey.
- On Saturday, the symposium's contest is announced. Whoever can best demonstrate "HOW TO COMMIT THE PERFECT MURDER" (10.71) wins.
- Lindsey's friends try to shield her, but she soon learns the truth. Then everybody learns whose sister she is.
- Samuel and Lindsey have sex for the first time under a rowboat sheltering them from a summer shower.
- Susie thinks, "In the walls of my sex there was horror and blood, in the walls of hers there were windows" (10.138).
- In heaven, they play "How to Commit the Perfect Murder" all the time. Susie's favorite weapon is the icicle, because it melts inside the body of the victim, leaving no trace.

Chapter 11

- Susie watches her dad get up around 4am every morning to walk Holiday. Every morning, he walks past Mr. Harvey's house.
- It's late summer, and there's still no progress on the case. Mr. Salmon dreams of killing him, but knows he'll need solid proof before it comes to that.
- Mr. Harvey is less and less worried about the police. They've almost completely stopped surveillance of him. And he makes sure to blend in and be on his best behavior so none of the neighbors begin to suspect him.
- He kills cats, dogs, and other small animals. The neighbors blame a mean kid, Joe Ellis, for their missing pets.
- He kills them, Susie realizes, to try to stop himself from killing another girl, like one of the school girls he can see and hear from his house.
- In August, the police can't take anymore of Jack Salmon's calls to the police station about Mr. Harvey. Len Fenerman comes over and tells him to stop.
- Jack realizes that Fenerman is stopping the investigation into Harvey, and that Abigail

agrees with everything the police say.

- That night, Jack sees a light in the cornfield from his window. He thinks it's Harvey. He gets his baseball bat and goes out there.
- Susie wishes she could tell him that's it's just Clarissa waiting for Brian in the field.
- When Mr. Salmon sees Clarissa, he runs at her, knocking her down, screaming, "Susie!" (11.113). Brian hears him and as he comes across the field, holding a torchlight.
- Susie, but nobody else, sees that Mr. Harvey is in fact in the cornfield.
- Brian shines the light on Mr. Salmon and Clarissa and freaks out. He throws Mr. Salmon off of her, then grabs Mr. Salmon's baseball bat and starts hitting him with it.

Chapter 12

- Jack Salmon's in the hospital now, and Detective Fenerman has figured out what happened. Jack will have to have knee surgery.
- Flashback to earlier the day. The Salmon family wakes to the sounds of the sirens coming to the cornfield and realize Jack isn't home.
- When Abigail finds out what happened, she rushes to the hospital, after forbidding Lindsey to come.
- Meanwhile, Lindsey calls Nate's mom, and arranges for her to babysit Buckley.
- Then she calls Hal Heckler and gets him to give her a ride to the hospital on his motorcycle.
- Hal waits for her while she visits her dad in his hospital room.
- Meanwhile, Fenerman arrives at the hospital. Abigail is pacing in a corridor, worried because Jack is in surgery.
- Fenerman finds her and they talk about what happened. They walk outside and Abigail bums a smoke from him. She learns that Fenerman's wife committed suicide. Eventually, they start kissing.
- Lindsey is asleep in her dad's room now, holding his hand.
- (Wait, we thought he was in surgery!)
- When Abigail and Fenerman come back from outside, Hal tells her Lindsey's in with Jack.
- Susie watches souls rising up from the hospital and the nursing homes. Franny taught her how to see them.

Chapter 13

- It's fall, 1974. Lindsey's back in junior high, now grist for the rumor mill. On top of being Susie's sister, she's also the daughter of the crazy guy.
- Clarissa and Brian are responsible for spinning that rumor. Good thing they're now at Fairfax High School.

- Ray and Ruth (also at Fairfax) listen to them talking nonstop about Susie and her dad, using it for popularity. Susie notes that Brian and Clarissa are now having sex.
- Buckley is in kindergarten now, and he's in love with his teacher.
- Abigail is internally rebelling against the monotony of household tasks and dreaming of Len Fenerman.
- Jack is back home, his knee healing, resisting his urge to go after Mr. Harvey.
- He plays with Buckley and Holiday in the yard, and he's set to go back to his accounting job on the 2nd, after Thanksgiving. He's isolating himself and feels Abigail drifting away.
- One day, Jack, Buckley and Holiday accidentally burst in on Lindsey in the bathroom. She's trying to shave her legs.
- After sending the boy and the dog away, Jack gives her some leg-shaving advice. They also talk about his suspicions of Mr. Harvey.
- Lindsey understands that if something of Susie's could be found at Mr. Harvey's house, that would help prove his guilt. She says, "So you'd want to be able to get into his house?" (13.81).
- He says, "You should finish shaving, honey" (13.83), but Lindsey understands what he's communicated to her. He wants her to do it.
- It's the Monday before Thanksgiving, and Grandma Lynn, watching Abigail do the dishes, realizes she's having an affair and makes her go for a walk with her.
- Lynn tries to make her give up the affair, but Abigail won't admit to having one.
- On the way home, Abigail smells "foreign cigarettes" (13.155) and follows her nose, while Lynn walks home.
- Abigail finds Ruana Singh smoking outside the Singh house. She bums one of her smokes and they talk.
- Ray is upstairs, reading and thinking of Susie.

Chapter 14

- Lindsey stakes out Harvey's greenhouse for seven days, stalking him the way he stalks others.
- She's trying out for the boys' soccer team, Samuel by her side, and can see the house from the field.
- Mr. Harvey watches her watching him and wishes the family would get off his case.
- It's happened before in other cities. He fools everybody, except some families.
- Lindsey sees that Harvey takes off for a couple of hours every afternoon. Susie's spies on him as he walks around Pennsylvania parks, watching the people with his "wild and bottomless lust" (14.9).
- November 26, 1974: Lindsey sees Harvey take off, and she fakes an injury on the soccer field.
- Then, she breaks into the greenhouse through a basement window.
- The floor plan is exactly like hers, and she's hit by family memories with each step she

takes.

- She sees Susie run past her and she chases her into the dollhouse room.
- All the other girls he's killed are here with Lindsey, too. Susie can see them, and she says their names and tells how they died. (See "Characters" for the gruesome details.)
- Lindsey finds Harvey's bedroom and goes in. She finds the sketchbook and hears a car.
- She finds the page Susie wants her to find. It's labeled "Stolfutz Cornfield" and it features a sketch of the underground hole, site of Susie's death.
- She rips it out while Mr. Harvey has a snack in the kitchen. Harvey hears boards creak and runs up the stairs.
- Lindsey opens a window and jumps out, just in time. He watches her running away, unharmed. The numbers on her soccer jersey, "5! 5! 5!" (14.51) flash dangerously at him.
- Lindsey gets home, surprising her mom, dad, and Grandma Lynn, announcing her successful break-in.
- Abigail doesn't want to hear it. She has Buckley to pick up, and Thanksgiving to cook.
- Jack is relieved and grateful to finally be believed. As he goes to make a call, Lindsey tells him that Harvey saw her.
- Afterwards, in heaven, Franny gives Susie a map to a place where she meets Harvey's other victims, and they listen to each other's stories.

Chapter 15

- Mr. Harvey's remembering shoplifting with his mother as a child. Sometimes they got caught.
- They robbed fresh roadside graves together.
- He realized early that being a woman and being a kid are "the two worst things to be" (15.24).
- When he first sees Lindsey running from his house he panics, but then calms down the way his mom taught him.
- He drops the bloody knife and his "trophy bag" (15.26) down a hole he'd drilled in the foundation. The he calls the cops and reports the break-in.
- Jack tries calling Detective Fenerman, but can't reach him. He learns the police are already at Harvey's.
- When Harvey fails to tell them about the missing drawing, they *almost* arrest him.
- But he pretends he didn't notice it missing, and shows them another drawing like it.
- He says he was trying to figure out how Susie had been killed, and he got the idea of the hole.
- The cops buy this, and tell him that Fenerman will come and ask him more questions later.
- Meanwhile, Abigail picks up Buckley, then stops at a pay phone to call Len Fenerman and tell him to meet her at the mall.
- At the mall, she lets Buckley stay at the supervised play circle, much to his joy.
- While the cops are questioning Harvey, she's following Fenerman down into the "inner

workings of the mall" (15.55).
- As they kiss, Mr. Harvey packs, Buckley makes a friend, Lindsey and Sam kiss, Lynn drinks, and Jack stares at the phone.
- Mr. Harvey splits town, while Abigail and Fenerman make love, Abigail's temporary respite from her broken heart.

Chapter 16

- On the first anniversary of Susie's death, she sees Ruana Singh beginning to realize that her husband is so devoted to his work that he's drifting away from her.
- Ruth comes over, introduces herself, and asks to see Ray.
- She has candles, and wants to have a vigil for Susie at the cornfield.
- Ruth and Ray often practice kissing together, and people think they're a couple, even though she thinks it should be obvious that she likes women.
- When they get to the cornfield, they find Samuel and Hal. Others have already come, left flowers, and gone.
- Neighbors can see them from windows, and they call others. Lots of people start showing up.
- As the sun goes down, the cornfield fills with people holding candles, singing dirges.
- Lindsey shows Abigail, but Abigail says she isn't interested in a memorial.
- Sensing her distance, Lindsey asks her if she plans on leaving them. Lying, she says she won't leave them.
- She holds Lindsey and then tells her to go tell Jack about the vigil.
- Buckley, Lindsey, and Jack go across to the neighborhood and join the growing crowd memorializing Susie.

Chapter 16: Snapshots

- When alive, Susie took lots of pictures of her family.
- Summer 1975, Abigail asks Jack to make love to her, and she leaves home.
- In the fall, Grandma Lynn calls Jack and says she's moving in.
- That December, Mr. Harvey has been gone over a year, and nobody has been able to find him.
- One cold day, Lindsey, gets a ride to the police station from Hal, hoping for information.
- At the station, she sees her mother's red scarf on Len Fenerman's desk, and she freaks out.
- When Fenerman comes around the corner, Hal and Lindsey realize Abigail was having an affair.
- When Buckley is seven he builds a fort for Susie, with Samuel, Hal, and Lindsey helping

him.

- He reads comic books in his fort and doesn't let himself wish for his mother.
- Fall 1976, Fenerman surveys the evidence against George Harvey, recovered from his house. He knows that Jack Salmon was right about Harvey, but, there is no record of Harvey anywhere.
- When he sees Susie's jingly pompom hat, he thinks of Abigail and his love for her.
- Susie feels sorry for Fenerman because he didn't solve the crime in time. He feels extremely guilty.
- Susie sees something he doesn't see – her keystone charm found near the bones of a child's foot, found by a hunter in Connecticut.
- In the spring of 1976 Abigail drives to California and gets a job at a winery.
- Ray gets handsomer and handsomer as the years go by, and he leaves for college.
- His mom packed the book of Indian poetry, and when he unpacks it in the dorm, Susie's picture falls out.
- Buckley plants a garden. Sometimes, Abigail calls home.
- Ruth moves to New York City. When she's not working, she roams the streets.
- When she sees a place where a dead girl was killed, she can see what happened.
- In December 1988, Fenerman learns that Susie's charm was discovered near the body of girl found in 1976.
- In 1982, Hal meets a biker whose mother, Sophie, was killed by her tenant, a dollhouse builder who matches Mr. Harvey's description. Hal calls Fenerman.
- And the years go by for Susie, collecting snapshots of her family and friends. When Holiday dies he comes to Susie's heaven.

Chapter 17

- When Lindsey is 21, she and Samuel are riding the motorcycle back from her graduation. They have matching spiky haircuts.
- About eight miles from their turn-off, it's raining so hard they have to pull off the road.
- They run to a Victorian house they find in the distance. It's abandoned, so they go inside. Samuel falls in love with the house and says he wants to buy it.
- Susie stops watching when they "unzip their leathers" (17.53) and the lightning and thunder stop.
- Jack, Hal, Lynn and twelve-year-old Buckley are back at the Salmon home, anxiously awaiting the return of Lindsey and Samuel.
- After Buckley tells Jack goodnight, he looks at the pictures Susie took. He finds some pictures of Abigail, one just as he's coming home from work, and another just after, when he's kissing her.
- He can see she's not wearing "the mask" (17.70) in the first picture, but wearing it in the second. He asks the picture, "Do I do that to you? How did that happen?" (17.71).
- Back at the abandoned house, Samuel asks Lindsey to marry him, and move into this

house with him while he restores it. She says yes. Up in heaven, Susie goes nuts with happiness.

- The motorcycle won't start, so Lindsey and Samuel run the eight or ten miles back to the Salmon house in their "underwear and T-shirts" (17.48). They'd smother running in their leathers.
- They burst into the house, tell their story, and announce their engagement. Everybody is overjoyed and they celebrate with champagne.
- During the celebration, Buckley sees Susie standing under the clock and almost says her name.
- As time passes, Susie gets bored and starts riding in Philadelphia trains, watching people, dreaming of her life before.

Chapter 18

- In New York, Ruth is talking to her dad on the phone. She learns that the sinkhole (where Susie's body parts were dumped) will be filled in so the area can be developed.
- Ruth has always been fascinated with the sinkhole and plans to go back and check it out soon.
- Since she lives in a tiny closet, in the house of a nosy lady, she stays out all the time.
- When she's not working in the bar, she wanders the streets, finding places where women and girls were murdered, writing about them in her notebook. The dead in heaven admire her work.
- Buckley, now in seventh grade, gets up early that weekend to work on his garden.
- When he comes out with a box of clothes, Jack stops him.
- Buckley says he needs the cloth to makes strips to tie his tomatoes to their stakes. Jack tells him that the clothes in the box belong to Susie.
- Buckley says he should be able to use them, but Jack tells him no way.
- Buckley gets mad, and tells his dad to get over Susie and be there for his living family. He accuses him of stealing Susie's Monopoly shoe.
- Buckley says Abigail left him because he couldn't get over it.
- Jack hears a voice inside him say, "*Let go, let go, let go*" and then his father collapses. Buckley runs to get Grandma Lynn.
- Jack has suffered a heart attack and is in the hospital. Buckley is in bed, consumed with guilt. He prays to Susie to save Jack.
- In heaven, Susie meets her father's father, and they dance together to Samuel Barber's " Adagio for Strings."

Chapter 19

- At the winery, Abigail finds a message for her from Lynn saying there's an emergency.
- She calls the hospital and learns of Jack's heart attack. She gets on the next plane to Philadelphia.
- At the stopover in Chicago she calls Lynn to tell her she's coming, and she looks at Susie's picture for the first time in eight years. She leaves the picture by a tree outside the airport.
- Samuel, Lindsey, and Buckley meet her at the airport. It's awkward. When Lindsey tries to talk to her, Abigail tells her, "I lied to you" (19.56).
- In the car, Buckley tells her, "Fuck you" (19.61), and she can see how angry he is.
- When Abigail sees Jack in the hospital room, she starts crying. He jokes that he had the heart attack to get her home.
- He tries to touch her face, but can't. So, she rests her check in his hand.
- Outside the hospital room, Lynn takes a message from Len Fenerman from the nurse, before she can take it in to Jack. It's a message saying he'll come see Jack soon, with well wishes.
- Lynn stashes the note in her purse.

Chapter 20

- While Jack and Abigail are reuniting, Mr. Harvey is at a shack in the woods in Connecticut.
- He once killed a waitress in there, buried her body under the ground, and used her tips to buy pants. Her grave has been dug up.
- Fenerman is holding the evidence bag with Susie's Pennsylvania keystone charm inside it. He wants to give it back to the Salmons even though it's against the rules. He heard Jack was in the hospital and thinks the charm will help him get well.
- Abigail buys flowers from a girl in the parking lot and brings them to Jack's room.
- Then, she goes to a diner and eats, deciding to go back to California after visiting Jack.
- Back at the hospital, about 10pm, she watches her sleeping husband and realizes how much she loves him.
- She falls asleep around midnight. Two hours later, the rain starts. It's also raining in Susie's heaven and in Connecticut where Harvey sleeps in the shack.
- He's dreaming of Lindsey in her soccer jersey, running from his house, as he always does when "he [feels] threatened" (20.36). Right now he feels very threatened.
- Two hours later Jack wakes up, thinks about Lindsey and Buckley, and watches Abigail sleep.
- Susie comes into the room, but she isn't sure if they will be able to see her.
- Abigail wakes up when Jack starts talking to Susie. She lies on the bed with Jack.
- He tells Abigail he thinks Susie was in the room. They make up, and she agrees to stay home.

- They kiss and cry together.

Chapter 21

- After the hospital, Susie watches Ray sleeping, and thinks of the first and only time he kissed her, by her locker at school. She wishes she could kiss him again.
- The next day, Ruth and Ray head for the sinkhole.
- Around the same time, Fenerman is going to the hospital and gives Jack and Abigail Susie's charm.
- He tells them that they've been able to connect Harvey with other murders. Abigail hadn't realized that Harvey actually is Susie's killer.
- She asks Fenerman to leave, and Jack thanks him for the charm.
- Next, Susie watches Mr. Harvey driving.
- He'd forgotten the girls and women he killed, but lately they are all coming back into his mind. Susie wonders when he'll remember her.
- Ray and Ruth watch the sinkhole, and Ruth tells Ray she wonders if Susie's body was dumped here. Susie cheers from heaven at Ruth's correct guess.
- Ruth feels Susie and talks to her.
- Susie can see Mr. Harvey driving on the road toward the Salmon house, and she can see Lindsey inside the house, alone.
- When he's almost there, a cop stops him, and asks him to leave the neighborhood, so he does.
- Ruth and Ray are standing next to Ray's car when Ray goes into some brush to pick flowers for his mom.
- Then, Mr. Harvey is driving toward the sinkhole, remembering that he'd put a dead body there.
- He drives past Ruth. She sees all the women he's killed, and then passes out.
- At the same time, Susie "[falls] to Earth" (21.161).

Chapter 22

- Ruth goes up to heaven, and Susie goes into Ruth's body. While Ray helps is helping Susie up, the people in heaven are throwing flowers at Ruth.
- Susie tells Ray to kiss her and he does, even though he knows Ruth doesn't seem like herself.
- She tells him to take her over to Hal's bike shop, which is closed right now. After kissing her again he drives her across the tracks to the shop.
- At the bike shop, Ray realizes that Susie is in Ruth's body. They make love and fall asleep.

- Susie wakes at sunset and then wakes Ray.
- She tells him that the dead are among the living, and that he can talk to her anytime he wants.
- She tells him to read Ruth's journals.
- Susie feels that her time in Ruth's body is coming to a close. She tells Ray she probably won't be able to come again.
- Then she calls home. Buckley answers the phone. She tells him it's her, but he can't hear her.
- She realizes that she's out of Ruth's body and Ruth is back in it.

Chapter 23

- The next morning Ray wakes up in his room, where he's curled up with Ruth, his world changed.
- Around three he had woken up and read Ruth's journal, with its details of murdered women and girls.
- At the hospital, Buckley is wheeling Jack out to the car followed by Lindsey and Abigail.
- Ruana is thinking about divorcing her husband when she hears Ruth and Ray moving about upstairs. When they come down, she gives them pie and coffee.
- Hal, Buckley, Lynn, and Samuel are at home, waiting for the newly reunited family to return from the hospital. Lynn has the champagne out for the occasion.
- Hal's brought a drum set for Buckley, an early thirteenth birthday present.
- Susie watches her family arrive home.
- When Lindsey and Abigail are getting Jack's bags from the trunk, Lindsey asks her mother if she'll hurt Jack again.
- Abigail says she'll try not to. Lindsey tells her she knows she had an affair with Fenerman.
- When Abigail gets into the house, she goes straight to Susie's old bedroom, to tell Susie she loves her, then joins the others downstairs.
- Over champagne, Samuel toasts everybody, and says how proud and happy he is to be marrying Lindsey, and he kisses her in front of everybody.
- Susie tells us, "These were the lovely bones that had grown around my absence: the connections […] that happened after I was gone" (23.79).
- Hal notices Ray and Ruana outside the house, dropping off a pie on the porch. He opens the door to invite them in.
- While Susie's loved ones enjoy each other's company, Ruth roams the cornfield, thinking of Susie.
- Later, Samuel tells Ray and Ruana about his plans to renovate the old Victorian house where he and Lindsey got engaged.
- Ray tells him that Ruth's dad owns the house. Samuel is amazed.
- And then Susie's stops watching.

Epilogue: Bones

- Grandma Lynn passes away several years later, but Susie hasn't seen her yet.
- Susie peeks at Earth only occasionally now.
- Samuel and Lindsey get married and Ruth's dad lets Samuel buy the old Victorian house, letting Samuel pay him in labor – he hires Samuel to be part of his renovation company.
- Samuel and Lindsey rough it while the house is being restored, and soon Lindsey becomes pregnant.
- Ray has become a doctor, and Ruth is still in New York, trying to find a way to express what she knows about the dead.
- Susie is in the big "H" Heaven now, and has lots of fun. You can have things in this Heaven that aren't available in others.
- One day, Susie and her Granddaddy are watching Earth. She sees Mr. Harvey get off a Greyhound bus, go into a diner, and order coffee.
- He notices a teenage girl, and follows her out behind the diner to the bus station.
- He looks at the deep ravine right in front of them and plans his next move.
- He tries to talk to the girl, but she blows him off and walks away.
- Susie notices that there are lots of thick icicles hanging over Harvey's head.
- Then one of those icicles falls, knocking Mr. Harvey off his balance and into the ravine, where his body won't be found until the snow thaws.
- Later, Susie watches Lindsey working in her garden. She watches Samuel bring their daughter, Abigail Suzanne, out to her.
- One day Susie sees a man showing his wife Susie's charm bracelet. He'd found it at the industrial park, recently bulldozed.
- His wife says, "This little girl's grown up by now" (Epilogue.37).
- Susie thinks, "Almost. Not quite," and wishes us "all a long and happy life" (Epilogue.38-40).

Themes

Theme of Mortality

In *The Lovely Bones* Susie Salmon recounts, from the afterlife, her grim and violent death by the hands of her rapist and neighbor, George Harvey. Susie says that the way we die, and the needs, desires, and qualities we possess at the time of death, impact our experiences in the afterworld. This is the story of Susie's experience in the afterworld, where she watches her family on Earth breakdown and rebuild. She also stalks her killer and tries to engineer his capture, while learning about his previous crimes and communing with his other dead victims.

Eventually, Susie comes to terms with her existence in the new realm. The novel contrasts a hideous death with a lovely and compelling vision of the afterlife.

Questions About Mortality

1. How do you feel about Susie's depiction of the afterlife?
2. If Susie had died of illness or accident, would her friends and family suffer in the same way? How might the circumstances of a person's death influence the way their loved ones deal with the loss?
3. What might happen to Mr. Harvey after he dies? Does he go to heaven or wide wide Heaven?
4. If you went to the afterworld today, what would it look like by the rules of Susie's cosmology? What wishes, desires, talents, interests, and unresolved issues would accompany you?

Theme of Love

As a vital counter to all the death and violence, *The Lovely Bones* offers us a tender vision of familial love, and a variety of love affairs and romances. We watch the uncomplicated love of super couple Lindsey (Susie's sister) and Samuel (her beau). And then there is the affair between Abigail (Susie's mom) and Detective Len Fenerman, who's in charge of Susie case. We also the crumbling and then reinvigorated love between Susie's parents. Things get really complicated when we talk about the love triangle of Susie (as a ghost), Ruth Connor, and Ray Singh (Susie's first love). Where Susie and her loved ones experience abundances of love, her killer is loveless and unloved.

Questions About Love

1. Does Abigail ever love Len Fenerman? Does Len love Abigail.
2. Is Lindsey and Samuel's relationship believable? Or is it too good to be true? Does Susie describe their relationship accurately, or is she biased by her own romantic notions?
3. Do you think Ray and Ruth will ever fall in love romantically? How would you describe their friendship?
4. Why does Clarissa lose her love for Susie after Susie dies?
5. Mr. Harvey seems incapable of giving or receiving love. If he hadn't died, would there be a chance to change this? Why or why not?
6. Abigail loves her family, yet she leaves them for eight years. How do we account for this seeming paradox?

Theme of Violence

The Lovely Bones makes no bones about it – it's a very violent book. It begins with Susie's brutal rape and murder by George Harvey and looks at his other crimes. This violence is also a violence against Susie's family, which nearly breaks apart under the strain of her death. *The Lovely Bones* stays focused on violence against women and girls, particularly those whose lives are taken by violent attackers.

Questions About Violence

1. Does the novel offer any explanations for the violence against women it depicts?
2. The the novel offer any clear explanations for why Harvey is the way he is?
3. Does the novel desensitize or resensitize readers to violence?
4. Is violence ever used positively in the novel? Is there even such a thing as positive violence?
5. What are some of the scenes that stand in counterpoint to extreme violence depicted?
6. Is there a connection between the breast-less, vagina-less anatomy model in Ruth's art class and the sexual violence in the novel? Why or why not?

Theme of The Supernatural

This is where things get fun. Whereas we know that the violent crimes in *The Lovely Bones* are reflections of brutal reality, the supernatural events of the novel leave us room to indulge our imaginations and dream of a beautiful beyond. Susie is definitely a nice kind of ghost. She's only mean to bad guys. Her powers are often limited to casting her reflection in glass surfaces and thinking hard about people to make them think of her. In all, the supernatural aspects of the novel give us some hope and a counterbalance the grimness of death. Such aspects also argue that it's important that we remember the dead, and discover and share the truths of their lives and death. Doing so helps them to forget about Earth and move on.

Questions About The Supernatural

1. How would you describe Susie as a ghost? Is she a stereotype? Why or why not? What are her powers? Her limitations?
2. Was it right for her to use Ruth's body to have sex with Ray? Why or why not?
3. Would you like to read more books with ghostly narrators? Why or why not? Is it harder to relate to Susie since she's not living?
4. Did Susie have a hand in Harvey's death?

Theme of Sex

Other than a single kiss and a few fantasies, Susie's rape is her first experience with sex. In *The Lovely Bones* Susie describes how her sexuality changes and grows after her death as she watches those she left behind in their sexual lives. Through Abigail's affair with Detective Len Fenerman and Len's frequent sexual encounters after Abigail, Susie learns that sex can be a way to forget, to stop time for a moment and keep the horrors of reality at bay. In the figures of Ray and Ruth, both utterly fixated on Susie after her death and both unclear about their sexual identities, sexuality is complicated and not necessarily fixed by gender. It doesn't even necessarily have to be between two living people. Whatever the sexual arrangement, the novel depicts consensual sex as a positive act, a means of developing and discovering identity. Always, consensual sex is held in contrast to the horrible rapes Mr. Harvey commits.

Questions About Sex

1. What are Abigail's motivations for sleeping with Len Fenerman? What are Len's motivations for sleeping with her?
2. How would you describe Ruth's sexuality? Ray's?
3. Is sex still important to Susie after she has it with Ray? Why, or why not? If she hadn't had sex with Ray, would she have been able to get over being raped and move on to the other Heaven anyway?
4. How does Susie's rape impact the way she views sex?
5. Is it OK that Samuel and Lindsey carry on a sexual relationship starting at age fourteen? Why, or why not?
6. What are some of the positive and negative representations of sex and sexuality in the novel?

Theme of Family

The Lovely Bones examines the opposite extremes of family life. On the one hand, we have the Salmons, a happy loving family with a stable life in the suburbs. On the other, we have Mr. Harvey, who is completely alone in the world and has never known a happy family moment. He infiltrates suburbia and uses it as a disguise for his dark plans – to destroy the happy family he envies. Yet, even the taking of the oldest child doesn't destroy the love the Salmon family shares. Much of the novel's power lies in its depiction of the breaking down and rebuilding of the Salmon family, the saga it undergoes after Susie's death. It also draws on the popular idea that in the afterlife we meet up with our loved ones. While Susie waits for the rest of her family to join her, she contents herself with her grandfather, who lives with her in heaven and helps her transition her existence away from Earth.

Questions About Family

1. What do we know about Mr. Harvey's childhood?
2. Do you think that Harvey is jealous of Susie's family life? Why or why not?
3. Should Abigail confess her affair to Jack? If she does, or if he finds out in some other way, will their marriage survive? Should Lindsey tell her father what she knows? Why, or why not?
4. Why does Abigail begin to resent her domestic role?
5. Why does Ruana Singh ponder divorcing her husband?
6. Does the novel idealize and romanticize family life? Is it justified in doing so?
7. How are the home lives of Mr. Harvey and Len Fenerman contrasted with that of the Salmons? What are the effects of the contrast?

Theme of Time

Susie's conception in time greatly expands once she exits Earth. She knows what time it is on Earth, but sees that each person is their own clock. When that clock stops, a newer deeper kind of time is revealed. Yep, good old eternity. For Susie, everything that happened to her on Earth is endlessly far and endlessly near her in time. *The Lovely Bones* also looks at how photographs preserve and reactivate moments from the past, rendering them useful for present existence. Furthermore, it argues that remembering the dead – through art, thought, and chronicle – is a vital human activity, which can make things much easier for those who are no longer in the Earthly realm.

Questions About Time

1. How does Susie's conception of time change after her death?
2. Are time and memory interconnected in the novel?
3. What is Ruth's relationship with time in the novel?
4. How does what Susie's murder change the nature of time for her family?
5. Why is it so important to Susie and the other murdered girls that they be remembered? Do you think it's important to remember the dead? Why or why not?

Theme of Rules and Order

The Lovely Bones takes a look at how the order and safety of a suburban neighborhood in the 1970s is utterly disrupted by Mr. Harvey's rape and murder of Susie Salmon. Harvey is the disruption of order personified. A serial rapist/killer Harvey destroys the order of the lives of his victims, their loved ones, and his neighborhood. Opposing him is Detective Len Fenerman, whose goal is to restore order, or at least the fantasy of it in the town. His lack of success in that

regard – his failure to recognize Harvey's guilt until it's too late – gives the novel a realistic feel. Life is disorderly, messy, and often seemingly unfair. *The Lovely Bones* doesn't try to tell us otherwise. Love, it argues, is all the order we can hope for, and to live in a loving way is sometimes all we can do when life turns chaotic.

Questions About Rules and Order

1. Do you think Harvey could receive treatment that would reform him? Why, or why not? If so, what might this treatment look like?
2. Do characters find order in chaos? Why, or why not? If so, in what ways? Is chaos ever represented as positive or healing? Why, or why not? If so, when?
3. Why do you think Alice Sebold chose to set *The Lovely Bones* in a suburban neighborhood? Why not put the main action in New York City?
4. How does Len Fenerman contribute to the order and disorder in the suburban Pennsylvania town where Susie lives?
5. If Harvey had been caught, what would have been a just punishment for him? Why?
6. If Harvey had been caught, could Fenerman and the Salmons prove he is a murderer? Do they have enough evidence?

Quotes

Mortality Quotes

I knew he was going to kill me. I did not realize then that I was an animal already dying. (1.91)

Thought: This quote obviously refers to the violence by which she dies, which heavily impacts her experience in the afterlife. It also suggests that her injuries, prior to Mr. Harvey killing her with the knife, are serious enough to kill her.

We had been given, in our heavens, our simplest dreams. (2.17)

Thought: *The Lovely Bones* strongly suggests that when we go to the afterlife, we bring along all our Earthly traits, and we continue to grow and change after we die.

"I could not have what I wanted most: Mr. Harvey dead and me living. Heaven wasn't perfect." *(2.39)*

Thought: Susie isn't in to the whole death thing whatsoever when she first gets to heaven, but she gets used to it one she's realizes how cool it is.

"It was an elbow. The Gilbert's dog found it." (2.70)

Thought: We don't know exactly how they knew this was Susie's elbow, or what shape it was in when they found it. It comes to symbolize Susie's death and to stand in for the rest of her bones, which are never found.

But when they held up the evidence bag with my hat in it, something broke in her. The fine wall of leaden crystal that had protected her heart [...] shattered. (2.115)

Thought: For some reason, the saliva-covered hat, which Mr. Harvey uses to gag Susie, is what convinces Abigail that Susie is dead. Why is this more convincing to Abigail than the elbow? Well, because she recognizes it. She made it. It's a psychological thing.

"All evidence points to your daughter's death. I'm very sorry." (2.131)

Thought: Some of the worst words a parent can hear.

A little strange, Fenerman thought, but it doesn't make the man a murderer . (5.51)

Thought: We wonder what it would have taken for Len to think someone was a suspect. If that someone was a seemingly respectable suburbanite, probably a heck of a lot. This also shows us that Len isn't one of those cops who uses 'gut feelings' to solve crimes.

"Susie is dead," he said now, unable to make it fit in the rules of any game. (5.137)

Thought: Susie even cries in heaven when Jack is trying to explain Monopoly and Susie's death in one fell swoop. We wouldn't blame you if you cried too.

Ruth smiled into her cup. "Well, as my dad would say, it means she's out of this shithole." (6.119)

Thought: Ruth, at least in this moment, thinks of death as a relief from the crappiness of life. Yet, she comes to understand that there is work to be done here, for the dead, which will give her a) entrance into heaven without dying, and b)major brownie points with the heavenites when

she does die.

Heading north on First, she could tick off all the places she'd formerly stopped and stood, certain that she'd found a spot where a woman or girl had been killed. (18.9)

Thought: Ruth, as a result of deep interest and being touched by ghost Susie, exists on a plane where she can understand these crime scenes. New York City becomes a map of the places where women and girls were killed. Like Susie, Ruth focuses on female victims.

A moment later, the icicle fell. They heavy coldness of it threw him off balance just enough for him to stumble and pitch forward. I would be weeks before the snow in the ravine melted enough to uncover him. (Epilogue.30)

Thought: We *feel* like Susie helped the icicle fall, but there's just no way to know! How frustrating. What do you think? What or who makes the icicle fall? Does it just fall by itself?

Love Quotes

My mother had been the one who knew the meaning of every charm on my bracelet – where we had gotten it and why I like it. She made a meticulous list of what I'd carried and worn. (2.47)

Thought: This intimate knowledge of the details of her daughter makes us feel Abigail's love for Susie. It also pleases Susie to no end, because she's in the phase of her ghosthood where being remembered and talking about is very important.

Yes, he had written Susie Salmon a love note. Yes, he had put it in her notebook […]. (2.100)

Thought: What a bitter pill! Susie doesn't even get to read her very first love note before she dies.

He christened the walls and wooden chair with the news of my death, and afterwards he stood in the guest room/den surrounded by green glass. (3.64)

Thought: Here Jack is shattering the ships in the bottles that Susie used to help him complete. His anger is an expression of his love, and he is afterwards able to see Susie's projected image in the glass.

He nodded and kissed my father's cheek. Something so divine that no one up in heaven could have made it up; the care a child took with an adult. (3.70)

Thought: This tender moment occurs just days after Susie's death. Throughout the novel, father and son are there for each other, though they have a few rough patches.

They had gone the week before to get haircuts at the same barber shop [...] and though Lindsey's hair was lighter and finer than Samuel's, the barber had given them identical short, spiky cuts. (17.8)

Thought: Isn't that the cutest thing! Samuel and Lindsey's are almost too romantic to be believed. They make it look easy, but they've worked hard for what they have.

He had been falling in love all over again. (17.67)

Thought: We doubt Jack ever fell out of love with Abigail. But looking at the pictures of his wife, candid photos Susie took of her, really makes an impact. In these photos, Jack sees through to the deeper Abigail, and this new understanding spawns this renewed love.

"No, I mean I love you, and I want to marry you, and I want to live in this house!" (17.75)

Thought: Another intensely romantic moment, conceived expressly for brightening Susie's day up in heaven. Seeing that her sister is having a happy life helps her let go of Earth.

He had been keeping, daily, weekly, yearly, an underground storage room of hate. Deep inside this, the four-year-old sat, his heart flashing. Heart to stone, heart to stone. (19.65)

Thought: It's the moment of Buckley's mother's return – a moment where love and hate blend for intense emotional impact on the part of the readers and, of course, for Buckley himself.

How could it be that you love someone so much and keep it a secret from yourself as you woke daily so far from home? (20.30)

Thought: Abigail realizes she's been blocking off her love for Jack. It takes the literal breaking, or at least attacking of his heart to reveal her true feelings.

I had taken this time to fall in love [...] – in love with the sort of helplessness I had not felt in death – the helplessness of being alive, the dark bright pity of being human. (22.146)

Thought: Susie is so darn wise and articulate now. She so sums up the old human condition. Our fragility leaves us open to the best and worst of human experience.

Samuel walked out to Lindsey then, and there she was in his arms [...] born ten years after my fourteen years on Earth: Abigail Suzanne, little Susie to me. (Epilogue.33)

Thought: The crowning symbol of love for Susie, a new Susie!

Violence Quotes

"I've made a little hiding place," said Mr. Harvey. (1.24)

Thought: The making of the trap, the luring Susie into it – these are not mere preludes to violence. But links in the chain of violence which culminates in her death.

"You aren't leaving, Susie. You're mine now." (1.69)

Thought: This act, forbidding Susie to leave, is overtly violent. He is no longer pretending to be nice. His words express the depth of the brutality that will swiftly come.

He reached into the pocket of my parka and balled up the hat my mother had made me, smashing it into my mouth. The only sound I made after that was the weak tinkling of bells. (1.81)

Thought: Although this is not the most violent thing Harvey does (if we can weight these things against each other) it's extremely impactful. Seeing him shut off her breath and voice gives the reader a vivid sense of suffocation.

I felt huge and bloated. I felt like the sea in which he stood and pissed and shat. I felt the corners of my body were turning in on themselves and out [...] (1.84)

Thought: Instead of the violence itself, we are seeing its impact on Susie in the moment. Her inner life has been, in a matter of moments, utterly transformed.

He had done this thing to me and I had lived. That was all. (1.90)

Thought: Susie has no illusions of continued life at this point. But, this sense of renewed life, of a moment of relief, is a powerful observation.

He had put me in a waxy cloth sack and thrown in the shaving cream and razor from the mud ledge, his book of sonnets, and finally the bloody knife […] tumbled together with my knees, fingers, and toes. (4.4)

Thought: The after-violence is incredibly striking. The idea of Harvey carving up her body and tossing it about so carelessly may be hard on the reader. We are glad her family was spared the knowledge. Or, would it have helped them to know the truth?

"If I'm not mistaken," said Miss Ryan, "there are no breasts on our anatomy model." (6.41)

Thought: Though this doesn't seem like a violent moment at first, but it sure feels violent to Ruth. Being denied the right to draw a part of her own anatomy is a type of violence, one thriving on power imbalances.

"This is not Susie, for Chrissakes," her mother would say, plunking down an inch thick sirloin in front of her daughter. (10. 8)

Thought: Ruth comes to equate Susie's murder with the slaughter of animals, so she becomes a vegetarian. Her totally insensitive mom provides a moment of comic relief.

It was on that day that I knew I wanted to tell the story of my family. Because horror on Earth is real and it is every day. It is like a flower or the sun; it cannot be contained. (14.100)

Thought: That horror Susie's talking about, most of it can be linked to some kind of violence – from Earthquakes to famine to cancer to murder.

The Supernatural Quotes

But I came to believe that if I watched closely, and desired, I might change the lives of those I loved on Earth. (2.39)

Thought: Much of Susie's earthly interactions are fairly subtle. She does lots of showing herself to people in glass, and she blows out a candle and maybe drops an icicle here and there. When she goes into Ruth's body and makes love with Ray, she's taking it to the next level.

"I was crossing through the faculty parking lot, and suddenly, down, out of the soccer field, I saw a pale ghost running toward me." (3.5)

Thought: When Ruth tells her mom this, she isn't sure she wasn't dreaming. But, she soon faces the fact that Susie did indeed touch her on the way out. And when you're touched by a ghost, you better take it seriously.

It was then that, without knowing how, I revealed myself. In every piece of glass, in every shard and sliver, I cast my face. (3.64)

Thought: After smashing up the ships in bottles, Jack gets to see Susie's face. It's then that he figures out that Mr. Harvey is her killer.

Had my brother really seen me somehow, or was he merely a boy telling beautiful lies? (7.35)

Thought: Susie has been trying not to think of Buckley too hard. When she thinks of people too hard, they might see her in the glass. There's a fine line between memory and imagination, and really seeing a ghost.

I listened to the sounds and felt the train's movements and sometimes, by doing this, I could hear the voices of those who no longer lived on Earth. Voices of others like me, the watchers. (17.104)

Thought: In this novel, the dead fill the world of the living. But they are restricted to the role of passive "watchers" that aren't involved in the living world (or not much, at least).

I had told people about her, what she did, how she observed moments of silence up and down the city and wrote small individual prayers in her journal, and the story had travelled so quickly that women lined up to know if she found where they'd been killed. (18.10)

Thought: Rose has some supernatural abilities. Stephen King might say she "shines." This makes her quite the celebrity in heaven, at least amongst women murdered in New York City.

"Someone came in the room and then left. I think it was Susie." (20.81)

Thought: Jack always embraces ghost Susie. He sees her like she sees herself – as someone who lives somewhere else, but can still come back and visit. Abigail has a much more guarded attitude toward the whole ghost thing.

On that same road where I had been buried, Mr. Harvey passed by Ruth. All she could see were the women. Then: blackout. (21.160)

Thought: Ruth's supernatural ability is just too much for her.

That was the moment I fell to Earth. (21.161)

Thought: Susie puts the "super" in supernatural. Here she's at the height of her realm switching powers.

"I've watched you both for years," I said. "I want you to make love to me." (22.125)

Thought: Susie is no cheesy succubus using humans for sex against their wills. No, Ray will only make love to Ruth's body when he learns Susie's inside it. It's consensual, and it seems to be a positive experience for him. For Susie, it's a chance to move past her brutal experience with Mr. Harvey and have a loving sexual experience. We get the feeling that now she can move on.

"We're here, you know […]. All the time. You can talk to us and think about us. It doesn't have to be sad or scary." (22.154)

Thought: Susie is saying that what we've been talking about as supernatural interactions between the living and the dead are really quite natural. What do you think?

Sex Quotes
I had been kissed once by someone I had liked. (1.76)

Thought: That kiss with Ray was the extent of Susie's sexual experience before Mr. Harvey.

It was not so much, she would write in her journals, that she wanted to have sex with women, but that she wanted to disappear inside them forever, to hide. (10.26)

Thought: Ruth is in the process of discovering her sexuality. The passage above is very personal to Ruth and not easily 'translated' to a concrete statement about her sexuality.

At fourteen my sister sailed away from me into a place I'd never been. In the walls of my sex there was horror and blood, in the walls of hers there were windows. (10.138)

Thought: When Lindsey and Samuel make love for the first time, Susie notes the vivid contrast between what Mr. Harvey did to her and what Lindsey and Samuel do with each other. Both are sex, but resemble each other only in the most basic way.

Clarissa, giggly with both fear and lust, had unlocked her privates and slept with Brian. However haphazardly, everyone I'd known was growing up. (13.2)

Thought: Susie gets awful snide when she describes Clarissa's sexual experience. Well, Clarissa, her best friend on Earth, has essentially betrayed her by not honoring her memory. Clearly Susie is jealous that others can experience consensual sex, while her only experience with sex was violent.

To find a doorway out of her ruined heart in merciful adultery. (15.66)

Thought: Susie recognizes her mother's right to chose what she does with her body. She seems to see Abigail's affair with Len Fenerman as a healthy, necessary part of her grieving process and her process of self discovery. What do you think?

What no one understood – and they could not begin to tell anyone – was that it had been an experiment between them. Ray had kissed only me, and Ruth had never kissed anyone, so […] they agreed to kiss each other and see. (16.17)

Thought: Ruth and Ray aren't going to let anybody dictate their path to sexual knowledge. But, they are both far less eager to actually have sex than the other people in the book. This undoubtedly has a lot to do with Susie.

Sex was an act of willful forgetting. It was the kind he made more and more in the rooms above the barbershop. (21.96)

Thought: Of course, Susie's talking about Len Fenerman, the lady-loving detective. He's using consensual sex to help him forget the vivid details of rape that come with his job. Do you think this is a healthy way to cope?

I held the part of him that Mr. Harvey had forced inside me. Inside my head I said the word gentle, and then I said the word man. (21.127)

Thought: For Susie, sex with Ray is a chance to face her fear of sex. The fear doesn't exist in heaven because up there she has no body. In Ruth's body, she gets to feel that unique trust that can happen between individuals during sex, a most vulnerable state.

Family Quotes

And they had never understood, as they did now, what the word horror meant. (2.45)

Thought: As a family, the Salmons were very innocent to the evils of the world. They viewed their suburban neighborhood as a safe place, where those with bad intentions can't enter.

The guilt on him, the hand of God pressing down on him, saying, You were not there when your daughter needed you. (5.3)

Thought: Family tragedies are known for producing spiraling guilt. Guilt is what you do when you can't do anything else.

[…] it was Lindsey who had to deal with what Holly called the Walking Dead Syndrome – when other people see the dead person and don't see you. (5.6)

Thought: Being Susie's sister becomes a much bigger part of Lindsey's identity after Susie dies. But only in the eyes of others. She remains her own person, dedicated to helping her family deal with the tragedy.

"Each year it's something I do for Leah. […] My wife. I'm a widower." (5.54)

Thought: One big reason Len Fenerman buys the widower lie is because he himself is a widower. It's doubtful Harvey knows this; he's just being his creepy self.

"You remind me of my wife," Len said. (6.199)

Thought: Nice pickup line, Len. Although Len is dedicated to keeping families safe from bad guys, he does take his own swipe at the Salmon family. Abigail initiates the affair, but Len makes early advances.

"You need to get yourself starved down, honey, before you keep fat on for too long. Baby fat is just another way to say ugly." (7.24)

Thought: Oh, Grandma Lynn. Sure she has some rather outrageous ideas, some body image issues, and she drinks a lot. But Lynn becomes vital to the Salmon's survival of tragedy, especially when she steps in to help after Abigail leaves.

"So you would want to be able to get into his house?" (13.81)

Thought: We were really disturbed by Jack encouraging his daughter to break into Harvey's house to get evidence of his guilt. Since this is a book, and Lindsey is one of the daring heroes of it, we'll let it slide.

It was on that day that I knew I wanted to tell the story of my family. Because horror on Earth is real and it is every day. It is like a flower or the sun; it cannot be contained. (14.100)

Thought: Susie is talking about the day she meets the other girls Harvey killed. She learns that by sharing her story with them, her pain lessens. So, if she can tell a big long story, her pain might disappear.

"Once upon a time there was a kid named Billy. He liked to explore. He saw a hole and went inside but never came out. The End." (16: Snapshots.45)

Thought: Buckley is working out the idea of death through art. He's also *showing* that he knows the details of what happened to Susie. Jack doesn't put it together though and puts the picture on the fridge with the drawing of the Inbetween. We can really see the depth of the pain of the family at that moment.

"We ran home for you, Mr. Salmon." (17.79)

Thought: And a good thing, too! Lindsey is a sensitive daughter, and she knows her dad could literally have a heart attack if she's too late and can't be found.

"Now I am in the place I call this wide wide Heaven because it includes all my simplest desires but also the most humble and grand. The word my grandfather uses is comfort. (Epilogue.15)

Thought: This Heaven, presumably, will eventually hold the whole Salmon family. But for now, Susie is quite content to hang out with her grandfather.

Time Quotes

I can still see the hole like it was yesterday, and it was. Life is a perpetual yesterday for us. (1.39)

Thought: At the end, we learn that Susie is telling her story from wide wide Heaven. So, it seems the hole is forever stamped in her memory. Now that she knows eternal time, the hole is both eternally far and eternally near her in time.

That was when we went to a part of heaven we didn't share. I missed her then, but it was an odd sort of missing because we knew the meaning of forever. (2.38)

Thought: She's talking about Holly, who remains a minor character. We like the quote because it challenges us to reflect on the nature of time, whether we agree with Susie's rather broadly painted conception of it.

I could not have what I wanted most. Mr. Harvey dead and me living. Heaven wasn't perfect. (2.39)

Thought: Susie does get both wishes, the first one for all eternity; the second for that time in the arms of Ray.

It was my first machine, my starter kit to becoming what I wanted to be. A wildlife photographer. (3.42)

Thought: Susie's first machine, her camera, also becomes a time machine, or the pictures she takes become one. The photos she leaves behind reanimate things that happened long ago -- so long as they exist and there is someone to look at them.

"If you stop asking why you were killed instead of someone else, stop investigating the vacuum left by your loss, stop wondering what everyone left on Earth is feeling [...], you can be free. (10.52)

Thought: Franny is a blunt intake counselor, if a bit mysterious. One point she's making: time is relative. The less Susie cares about her life on Earth, the further Earth and the memories are from her in space-time.

She couldn't stop the memories from slamming into her. (14.24)

Thought: We talk about this in "Setting." Since Harvey and the Salmon's houses have the same floor plan, time and space bends hideously for Lindsey. She is assailed in an almost physical way by memories of Susie at home.

Woosh and you can start over again. Or was life more like the horrible game in gym that has you running from one side of an enclosed space to another, picking up and setting down wooden blocks without end? (16: Snapshots.73)

Thought: Abigail's vision of what life *might* be about, sound a lot like Sisyphusian Hades (Sisyphus being the guy who has to keep rolling the boulder up the hill for all eternity). What do you think Abigail's vision of life looks like at the point we leave her in the book?

He saw me standing under the rustic colonial clock and stared. He was drinking champagne. There were strings coming out from all around me, reaching out, waving in the air. (17.103)

Thought: Aha! Clocks and time go together like ticks and tocks. Susie even describes herself as resembling a clock, with funny wavy arms, like her funny wavy conception of time.

Let go. Let go. Let go. (18.75)

Thought: This is what Jack Salmon hears before he has his heart attack, when Buckley begs him to forget Susie. Where does the voice come from? Is it Susie? Is it something within Jack?

After eight years it was, even for my mother, like the ubiquitous photo of a celebrity. (19.30)

Thought: When Abigail leaves Susie's photo outside the airport, it makes us tear up. We don't want her to give Susie up, but we know that she must. And Susie is already in heaven. Looks like we too have some letting go to do.

Rules and Order Quotes

"Nothing is ever certain," Len Fenerman said. (2.43)

That was the line my father said to my mother, "Nothing is ever certain." (2.44)

Thought: Len's phrase is comforting at first, but hollow and even cruel eight years later, when he brings them Susie's charm. It also shows his desire to maintain order in the chaos.

"I'm certain there's a man in my neighborhood who knows something." (5.29)

Thought: And so Jack's frustrating and fruitless attempt to bring his daughter's killer to justice begins. He's trying to restore order to the situation. But Len Fenerman's desire to preserve order by being carefully not to accuse people without evidence wins out.

A little strange, Fenerman thought, but it doesn't make the man a murderer . (5.51)

Thought: Len Fenerman is trying to be a good cop. He can't stand the idea of making a mistake, of inconveniencing an honest citizen. He's too careful.

"Each year it's something I do for Leah. [...] My wife. I'm a widower." (5.54)

Len felt that he was intruding on this man's private rituals. (5.55)

Thought: And here's where Harvey gets him. Since Len actually is a widower, Harvey inadvertently presses his sympathy buttons. Len will believe anything now, even a wedding tent.

I realized how subversive Ruth was then, not because she drew pictures of nude women that got misused by her peers, but because she was more talented than her teachers. (6.64)

Thought: Ruth is a triple threat – talented, opinionated, and willing to act. She's a threat to the order being imposed on her art class since the hippie art teacher got fired.

"You have to give up on Earth." (10.52)

This seemed impossible to me. (10.53)

Thought: Susie is still running on Earthly rules and order when she gets to heaven. She can't yet conceive of a the much broader design of the afterworld.

"5! 5! 5!" (14.51)

Thought: Lindsey's soccer jersey flashing at him as she escapes his clutches with evidence of his crimes represents the destruction of Harvey's ability to blend into society. It puts him on a path to deeper disintegration. Yet, it is not, for him, a reminder of what he did to Susie.

"Well, that person who did it had built something underground, a hole, and then I confess I began to worry about it and detail it the way I did the dollhouses, and I gave it a chimney and a shelf, and, well, that's just my habit." (15.38)

Thought: This is just a bit too much. If we were the cops, we would have arrested him then and there. We can't blame Len for this one. Oh, yes we can, he was at the mall with Abigail. Oh well, if Susie doesn't hold it against him, neither do we.

He wanted to give the charm back to my father from the first moment he was able to confirm it was mine. Doing so was breaking the rules, but he never had a body for them [...]. (20.6)

Thought: Len's gesture is appreciated, at least by Jack. Again, we see him trying to create order in a disorderly world, even if it means not going by procedure. Of course, he's also hoping to disrupt a little order here, too. He probably wouldn't mind if Abigail chose him over Jack.

But she was no shadow of a human form, no ghost. She was a smart girl breaking all the rules.

Thought: Ruth goes all gothic superhero on us at the end – breaking through the Inbetween, entering heaven, and leaving her body on Earth for Susie. Quite a feat, and an act of both defiance and preservation of order.

Study Questions

1. If you knew Mr. Salmon, would you take his suspicions of Harvey seriously, or not?

2. Is *The Lovely Bones* destined to be a classic? Why or why not? Should it be taught in school?
3. Could this novel be helpful to victims of rape, their loved ones, or the families of people with a murdered member? Why, or why not.
4. Why don't the police suspect Mr. Harvey?
5. If you were a psychiatrist, how would you analyze Mr. Harvey? Is there a cure for his problem? What might it look like?
6. How does Mr. Harvey compare to other serial killers you've seen in movies or read about in other books? How is *The Lovely Bones* different from or similar to other fictional stories about serial killers?
7. Does Susie have any sympathy for her killer? Do you?
8. Why don't critics like the film adaptation of the book? Do you like it? Why, or why not?

Characters

Susie Salmon Character Analysis

Susie is the hero and the starring ghost of *The Lovely Bones*. She's only fourteen when she's beaten, raped, and murdered by her neighbor, Mr. Harvey. She tells us her story from the afterworld. Part vengeful ghost, part wise sage, part hyper-romantic and sexually frustrated teen, Susie provides a fresh (though definitely ghostly) perspective on Earthly happenings, and on how the dead and the living interact.

Live Susie's Talents and Dreams for the Future

When Susie is on Earth, her dreams are fairly typical for a well-adjusted, talented girl. High school is the big deal in her immediate plans. In her Earthly life she sees the mediocrity of junior high fading into the past, as she becomes the queen of high school. This is why, in her first heaven, "all the buildings looked like suburban [...] high schools build in the 1960s" (2.1).

She is a natural with the camera, and learns from photographing her mother, Abigail, that a photo can reveal a person's inner needs and desires. The photos of her mother that Susie leaves behind help her father, Jack, to understand Abigail. This understanding leads to a strengthening of their relationship. Susie carries this photographic eye with her into heaven, and she often tells her story pictorially, as stressed in one of the few titled chapters, "Snapshots."

Susie is obsessed with design and arrangement. She sees the elements of the world as bones, or pieces of structures in the process of being built. The photos she leaves behind, Len Fenerman's photos of the dead, and all the metaphorical photos she takes from heaven are potent, overlapping structures within the body of the novel. As she moves through time in the afterlife, her perceptions become keener. Thus offering us with the fascinating idea that our

talents and interest continue to grow after we die.

Susie and Mr. Harvey, Foils

In *Lucky*, Alice Sebold's nonfiction account of being raped and the aftermath, she says, "I share my life with my rapist. He is husband to my fate" *(Lucky*, p. 53). There is a similar connection between Susie and Mr. Harvey. The magnitude of their horrid encounter ensures a seemingly eternal link. Plus, they are opposite ends of the axis around which the story revolves. Remove either one, and there is no story.

Susie is everything Harvey wasn't as a child – loved, happy, and safe. Bizarrely, he creates an imitation of Susie's suburban life. He has the same house she has, and he looks kind of like he belongs in her world. They even share the same bedroom in their respective homes. In fact, his appearance is a disguise he'll use to *foil* all of Susie's plans to continue her life. Similarly, she, ultimately, foils his plans to keep destroying girls, and by extension the families they come from.

As noted below when we discuss Susie as a tragic hero, the fact that Susie and Mr. Harvey share an interest in building, design, and structure is part of why he is able to victimize her. Some other girls might have run, and fast, the moment he started talking about the weird hole in the ground he built. This shared interest is also why Susie is able to understand and describe her killer so vividly. She is the sane to his psycho, and while she never understands precisely *why* he does what he does, she understands how he looks at the world.

Although they are both enraptured by building and design, their visions ultimately diverge. For Susie, everything is material to be shaped and designed positively. For Mr. Harvey, his interest in building is only to further his urge to tear down, break apart, and dispose of the structures (girls, families) he sees in the world.

Tragic Hero

If Susie was a nonfictional victim, we would never talk about her as a tragic hero with fatal flaws. But, since she's a character in a book, and she presents herself to us as just such a figure, we have no choice. So let's go through some of the key elements of a tragic hero and see how she fits the mold.

Too nice...In *Poetics* Aristotle argued that the hero in a tragedy should be an exceptional person, but with certain character qualities that lead him/her to make certain choices that result in his/her tragic end. In this case, Susie's so-called tragic flaws are trust, politeness, and curiosity.

Susie's curiosity about design, structure, and building make her easy prey for Mr. Harvey. She tells us (like *Alice in Wonderland* gone wrong), "I was no longer cold or weirded out by the look he had given me. It was like I was in science class: I was curious" (1.34). Curiosity alone couldn't get her into that hole. Innocence, trust, respect for authority, and politeness were also involved. Susie was acting within the rules, norms, and expectations of her culture.

Mr. Harvey is a neighbor, and her dad even called him "a character" (1.41) to explain his eccentric behavior. Susie and her parents have no idea that people like Harvey even exist, at least not in their very own neighborhood. So, Susie has nothing but a slight intuition to warn her of Mr. Harvey. But her curiosity, innocence, and trust in adults in general override that intuition.

*Already dead..*Now, Susie is also markedly different from most tragic heroes. They usually meet their end near the close of the stories they exist in. We could look at *The Lovely Bones* as Hamlet-type revenge tragedy, but with the end and the beginning switched. For most of *Hamlet* the ultra-introspective Hamlet wants revenge for his father's death. And at the end he dies (by poison-tipped sword to be exact).

Susie, on the other hand, is murdered at the beginning of *The Lovely Bones*. Like Hamlet, she spends the bulk of the tale being introspective, and seeking (and ultimately finding) revenge for her own and the other victims' deaths. This becomes a rather mature type of revenge, with the main goal of stopping Harvey from hurting other women, rather than making him 'pay' for his crimes.

What's the point? In classical literature the tragic hero might exist in part to instruct us on the danger of things like pride, vengefulness, or what have you. *The Lovely Bones* is more about showing us the beginnings of a cultural shift. After crimes like Mr. Harvey's became more known, schools, the media, parents, policeman, and politicians would warn us against the kind of trust Susie exhibits. "Don't talk to strangers" would take on a whole new meaning.

But, there is always somebody out there reinventing the game. There's no list of things to not do that will guarantee our safety. In the 2000s, such predators have the Internet at their disposal even. So, until/unless a time comes when we stop producing such predators in our society, we will continue adapting to try to keep ourselves safe. Keeping open a frank dialogue, like *The Lovely Bones* does, is vital for self/other-defense, and possibly, toward a world where people do such things less and less.

Susie's Focus on Female Victims

If you were from another planet and you read *The Lovely Bones* you might conclude that males are never the victims of violent sexual attacks and murders. Of course, we (and author Alice Sebold) know this is not the case. See, Susie is a very focused sort of ghost. We are all intrigued by people we can relate to. Susie can relate to those who are, or could be, like her. She might even consider it a personal responsibility to try to avenge victims who resemble her and to try to protect other girls who could end up like her.

Actually, Susie becomes an expert in the area of female victims (as does Ruth) and she is sharing what she knows. The story is told in the past tense, except for a few important moments. In the final chapter, Susie goes into present tense: "Now I am in the place I call this wide wide Heaven" (Epilogue.15). This suggests that she's telling *us* the story, now, from big

"H"-Heaven. In fact, the final (present tense) line of the story is directed right at us, the readers: "I wish you a long and happy life." We Earthlings are her audience. Only after she matures to the wide wide Heaven is she ready to tell us her story.

Susie and Sexuality

Throughout the novel, Susie offers fresh, candid perspectives on sex and sexuality. As in all things, she has the opposite attitude toward sex as Mr. Harvey. Susie sees sex as a beautiful and healthy human activity – so long as it's consensual. Before Mr. Harvey, her direct experience with sex consists of a single kiss with Ray. Since she was fourteen and in the throes of her late junior high era, she's curious about sex. She's aware of herself as an object of desire, even to Mr. Harvey when she encounters him in the cornfield. She says,

I'd had older men look at me that way since I'd lost my baby fat, but they usually didn't lose their marbles over me when I was wearing my royal blue parka and yellow elephant bell bottoms . (1.26)

But, she certainly doesn't see herself as a potential rape victim. As she tells her story, she switches back and forth between depicting the consensual sexual relationships of her loved ones, and Mr. Harvey's previous rapes. When she watches Lindsey and Samuel make love for the first time, she says,

At fourteen my sister sailed away from me into a place I'd never been. In the walls of my sex there was horror and blood, in the walls of hers there were windows. (10.138)

Even Abigail and Len Fenerman's affair is represented sympathetically by Susie. She sees it as part of her mother's process of healing and self-discovery. As she matures in the afterworld, not getting to experience healthy sex becomes a huge regret, and something that holds her back from renouncing Earth. Since Ruth is a virgin, and she lets Susie use her body to make love with Ray, it's like Susie is a virgin again and gets a chance to experience sex in a loving way. The novel does a pretty fabulous job of contrasting the extremes of healthy and unhealthy sexual relationships.

Mr. Harvey Character Analysis

Mr. Harvey is a sexual predator, a rapist, a serial killer. He's the 36-year-old neighbor who rapes and murders Susie, within minutes of her own home. Although indispensable to the novel, his story is always secondary to the stories of Susie and her loved ones. After Mr. Harvey leaves Susie's suburban neighborhood, she doesn't watch him as closely, unless he's thinking about Lindsey, or moving back toward her family. Susie is subtle but clear that he carries on his brutalities after her death, but if she sees his hideous acts, she doesn't do much reporting back on them.

It's a much-noted fact that Harvey is revealed as Susie's killer from the first pages. This is a

powerful use of dramatic irony. The readers are Susie's confidants, privy to the secret she wishes wasn't secret. We watch along with her in suspense for Harvey's guilt to be made known. Susie's constant use of the title "Mr." to refer to her rapist is disconcerting, but it pushes home the point that she viewed him as an authority figure, someone to be trusted, and if not trusted, obeyed.

Builder and Destroyer: Mr. Harvey's Past and Present
"According to the experts, there is no common thread tying serial killers together—no single cause, no single motive, no single profile." (source: FBI report on serial murder)

Susie can see into Harvey's past and she tells us some of what she sees. We learn that his mother was a desperate woman who taught Harvey to shoplift and even rob victims of roadside fatalities from alongside the road. At some point Harvey's father abandons his mother in Truth or Consequences, New Mexico. His family, before and after his mother disappears from it, seems pretty transient.

As a kid, Harvey is ashamed that his father doesn't have a 'normal' job. He can't tell people that his father "[works] in the desert [building] shacks of broken glass and old wood" (8.3). Still his father passes along his knowledge of building to his son. We can see that Harvey's father is an abusive person, but aren't given details.

We can say, with certainty, that Harvey's childhood was almost the complete opposite of Susie's. In Harvey we see a yearning for an idealized home, and family, in his chosen profession: building dollhouses, idealized homes in miniature. His success gives him what his father's building couldn't, financial security. Harvey makes enough to buy that family home in the suburbs, but he has no intention of filling it with a family of his own. Rather, it becomes the disguise which allows him to infiltrate the world he covets.

There are lots of allusions to *Othello* in the novel. *Othello*, unlike Harvey, is a largely sympathetic character, whose jealousy is fanned by the evil Iago, until he allows it to overcome him, and he murders his beloved wife. Since none of the other characters in *The Lovely Bones* exhibit jealousy or murderous tendencies, we can think of the allusions as clues pointing to jealousy as a motivator for Harvey's hideous behavior. He can't have the idealized, loving home and family, so he builds structures that allow him to infiltrate and attack it.

Serial Killer: Mr. Harvey's Crimes
Mr. Harvey's been living in the neighborhood for a few years at least, and Susie seems to be his first human victim from the neighborhood. According to Susie, Harvey's been staving off his urges by killing cats and dogs. In the novel, the phrase "serial killer" isn't used, because in the early '70s, it hadn't yet become a part of the popular vocabulary. We call him a serial killer because he fits the usual definition. As opposed to murderers and spree killers, serial killers are known for having 'cooling off times' – time in between attacks. Attacks are risky, big events, not every day happenings.

If the list of the dead we get in Chapter 14 is complete, Harvey kills a woman and a girl in 1960 (when Harvey would have been about 23), one girl in 1963, a teen girl in 1967, a teen in 1969, another teen girl in 1971, and then Susie in 1973. We later learn that "The first girl he hurt was by accident" (21.100). Susie tells us that, "He had regretted it, this quiet muffled rape of a childhood friend, but didn't see it as anything that would stay with either of them" (21.100).

We aren't given many details about Harvey's post-Susie victims. But when Harvey visits the shack in Connecticut in 1981, we are told that he killed a "young waitress [...] several years before" (21.1).We notice that there are years in between most killings, and other than 1960, no more than one killing per year. These gaps between killings are part of why Harvey is able to avoid detection.

If we examine the list of the dead in Chapter 14, we can also see that other than Sophie a landlord/lover, his victims were first very young girls, then progressively older teens, and then the waitress.

But, you'll have to make what you want out of that. We don't have enough reliable information or expertise in serial killers to make a whole lot out of the information. Plus, we have to be careful using anything we read about Mr. Harvey to generalize about actual serial killers. Otherwise, the FBI might get upset with us. The FBI says,

Serial killings are rare, probably less than one percent of all murders. They do, however, receive a lot of attention in the news and on screen—and much of the information out there is wrong. Yet, the public, the media, and even sometimes law enforcement professionals who have limited experience with serial murder, often believe what they read and hear. And this misinformation can hinder investigations. (source)

Dreams and Memories
Susie tries to show us that Mr. Harvey might be clear and calculating in his attacks on girls, but doing these acts isn't something he can easily deal with afterwards. She even comes to believe that he tries to stop himself – one explanation for why there is some time between attacks. Of course, he never tries to get help, or anything like that. Susie doesn't ever make excuses for what he does, but she does try to show us some of what goes on inside his head.

Interestingly, one thing that pushes him to strike again is his dreams. So long as he's having dreams about beautiful buildings, like the ones he has *after* a kill, he can keep the urges at bay. But, then the "*not still* dreams" (8.2) in which his desires to hurt women and girls come out, and the urges come back.

When we see Mr. Harvey eight years down the road, he has deteriorated further. Susie says that the "edges of Mr. Harvey seemed oddly blurred" (21.91). He no longer has a fixed residence, a stable profession. He no longer has a disguise of normalcy. Somehow, he's been

able to block off "the memories of the women he killed but now, one by one, they were coming back" (21.9), though he doesn't yet remember Susie.

Strangely, he sure remembers Lindsey though. If it hadn't been for her, he might've stayed there in the neighborhood for years to come. So, she's become as symbol of threat. Dreams and memories of her also seem to be the catalyst for his renewed memory.

Jack Salmon Character Analysis

Jack, Susie's dad, is the frustrated hero of the piece. He's the loving father who knows the truth of his daughter's murder, but can't prove it. His struggle is perhaps most poignant. He sticks it out every inch of the way, facing the truths of his world, and trying to keep his loved ones and himself from going mad over what's happened to Susie. He even manages, to some degree, to hold down his accounting job. Like the rest of the family (excluding perhaps Abigail) he believes in Susie's ghostly projections and listens to what she has to say. He, like Ruth, is comfortable with the idea of the dead and living coexisting.

Like Susie, he's a distinct foil for Mr. Harvey. While Jack's journey is a process of rebuilding and recovery (to whatever extent possible), Mr. Harvey's is one of disintegration and decay. Also, think of the bizarre moment when Jack is overcome with vengeance and almost attacks Clarissa in the cornfield, thinking she's Harvey. He almost inadvertently becomes a version of Harvey, a man who hurts young girls. Clarissa and Brian sure see it that way and use it to gain popularity among schoolyard gossips.

So, yes, Jack Salmon is something of a whipping boy. He gets taunted by his daughter's killer, baseball batted by Brian Nelson, cheated on, and heart attacked, in that order. He's also not perfect. In a disturbing moment, he all but begs Lindsey to break into Mr. Harvey's house. And because he can't bring himself to overtly involve her in such a dangerous thing, she goes it on her own. He doesn't pretend to be aghast when she brings back the proof, but thanks her sincerely. Man, if Harvey had gotten her, Jack would have probably died of guilt.

Interestingly, Jack never learns of Abigail's affair with Len Fenerman. What's more important is that Jack learns, in Abigail's absence, a lot more about who she is. This strengthens his love for her and gives him the knowledge he needs to develop a deeper relationship with her when she returns.

Abigail Salmon Character Analysis

Abigail is Susie's mom and a complicated woman. Her love for Susie is apparent in her intimate knowledge of things Susie related, as detailed to Len Fenerman. But, as Susie had already learned from photographing her mother, the role of perfect wife and mother was something of a disguise, masking other desires that rebelled against domesticity.

When Abigail learns Susie is dead, she can no longer keep up the façade. She becomes an adulteress (to get all *Scarlet Letter* on you) and then an abandoner of her family. Susie can relate to her mom in both instances. She recognizes her mother as an independent person, with the freedom to make her own lifestyle choices. She understands that her mother has her own way of dealing with grief, loss, and figuring out what she wants. Jack, Susie's dad, is likewise understanding of Abigail (though he doesn't know of the affair).

But Lindsey and Buckley, not so much. Of course, it's easier to have your mom leave home if you're dead than if you're alive, grieving, and very much in need. Chances are Abigail wouldn't have been the mother they imagined in their fantasies.

She returns eight years later after eight years, after Jack has a heart attack, and she is able to see how much she's loved Jack all along. She's learned about herself while she's been away, and she's learned about him as well. Ironically, only when he's laid low from the heart attack does she realize how strong he is and how strong he's had to be with her gone.

Lindsey Salmon Character Analysis

Lindsey, Susie's little sister, is thirteen when Susie dies. She is the living hero of the story Susie is watching and telling. Her story begins in winter in chaos, and ends in spring in reunion, marriage, and even a cute little bambino. She doesn't seem to have any bad qualities or even flaws, except, perhaps, being a tad too hard on Abigail. (But who can blame her?)

Although Susie is smart, Lindsey is considered a genius. She's not only a brainiac, but also one of the most physically fit people we know, able to run eight miles in the rain and leap from a killer's window in a single bound. Susie gets so caught up in Lindsey's life, especially the romantic aspect, that she almost thinks she's Lindsey sometimes. Late in the novel, Susie says, "I collected my college diploma and jumped on the back of Samuel's bike […]" (17.1). But, then she clarifies, snapping out of her fantasy:

Okay, it was Lindsey. I realized that. But in watching her I found I could get lost more than with anyone else. (17.2)

Through Lindsey, Susie can live her Earthly fantasies and eventually gain enough satisfaction to move on to deeper, more heavenly desires.

Lindsey, Running, and Jack

Yes, Lindsey stars in two very different scenes of running. In one, she's running for her life, away from Susie's killer. In the other, she's running freely, abandoning herself to the romance and joy of her life. In both scenes, Lindsey is running toward the same thing: home. In both scenes, she has the same ultimate goal: getting home safely to give Jack Salmon, in particular, the good news. Lindsey's relationship with her father is extremely touching.

After Susie's death, she becomes increasingly protective of Jack, and she even switches places with him, metaphorically, in the critical break-in scene. She knows that Jack is defeated in his attempts to prove Harvey's guilt, and she steps in to do the job for him. The break-in is also for Susie. Lindsey's being in Harvey's house reveals his other victims to her. Susie needs to know what he's done, in order to be able to be in commune with the other girls and, eventually, to move on.

Lindsey's Sexuality

Lindsey also turns some stereotypes on their heads. Like Abigail, Lindsey finds comfort in consensual, romantic sex, the opposite of what Susie experiences. Like Abigail's affair, Lindsey sexual relationship with Samuel could be considered wrong. She is only fourteen, after all, when she begins having sex. But, Lindsey and Samuel seem to have handled it responsibly. Through Lindsey (in part), Susie's finds beautiful contrast to the brutality of her sexual experience with Mr. Harvey.

Buckley Salmon Character Analysis

Buckley is Susie's little brother, the youngest Salmon child. He's about four when Susie is killed. Susie had a warm and close relationship with Buckley and even saved his life when he was chocking on a twig (in a somewhat improbable scene involving Susie driving him to the hospital).

Buckley believes in Susie's ghostly ability to show herself, to communicate with the living, and he sees her several times. But, he also comes to resent her parents' inability to get over her. Who can blame him? A father obsessed with a dead daughter, and an absent mother is just no fun. Luckily, he has Lindsey, Samuel, Hal, and Lynn to be there for him. And, eventually he gets his mom and dad back too.

Detective Len Fenerman Character Analysis

Fenerman (in the movie played by Michael Imperioli of *Sopranos* fame) is the detective in charge of Susie's case and a recent widower. He's part of the novel's love triangle; he has an affair with Susie's mom.

He lets Susie's killer get away. Yet, early in the novel, Susie says, "I still thank God for a small detective named Len Fenerman" (1.45). Why is she such a fan? For one thing, she feels sorry for him. But, that's not enough to account for it. OK, the quickest way to get on Susie's good list is to think about her, remember her, and care about her. She's even mad at Harvey for not remembering her. But Fenerman does. She is a part of his life, and he'll never forget her. That's why she has a soft spot for him in her ghostly heart.

Failure

I felt sorry for him. He had tried to solve my murder and he had failed. He had tried to love my

mother and he had failed. (16: Snapshots.50)

Fenerman is not the brilliant detective who solves the crime. Nor is he the bumbling detective who makes tons of mistakes, but nonetheless manages to solve the crime. No, Fenerman is a very human figure and is marked by failure, from the suicide death of his wife (which he, not we, might consider his fault), to his failure to suspect Mr. Harvey, to his failure to win Abigail's love.

He fails to solve Susie's crime for the very reason he's what we might call a 'good' cop. He doesn't want to treat Mr. Harvey unfairly, doesn't want to violate his civil liberties. He acts in such a way as to preserve the rights of ordinary citizens from unlawful search. OK, this is a tad thin – Fenerman could have done a better job. He could have taken Harvey in for questioning, found an excuse to search the house, etc. Fact is he simply didn't figure Harvey for the killer, and he was distracted.

First, Lindsey does what he was too reluctant to do – break into Harvey's place and find the evidence. If he hadn't been making love to Susie's mom in the underbelly of the mall, he would have gotten Jack's call, and arrived in time to arrest Harvey. But, knowing Fenerman, he might even have botched that. In spite of his failure, we like him, just like Susie does, because he's a decent guy, trying to protect those who can't protect themselves.

Fenerman's Love Life
OK, it isn't very nice having an affair with the married mother of the murdered girl you are investigating. But, according to Susie, this was something necessary for her mother. Susie says that for her mother making love with Fenerman is "a doorway out of her ruined heart" (15.66). In any case, Abigail basically uses him. He doesn't seem to mind, but wishes it could have turned into something more.

As with so many of the characters, Susie sees Fenerman's frequent post-Abigail sexual liaisons in his room over the barbershop as part of his process of understanding life, of dealing with the ugly world he's faced with in his work. As we seen throughout the novel, this consensual sex as a move toward understanding is presented as a sharp contrast to Harvey's violent sexual mode. Susie understands this about Len Fenerman and sees herself as acting similarly. She says,

I had come to both pity and respect Len in the years since my mother left. He followed the physical to try to understand things that were impossible to comprehend. In that, I could see, he was like me. (20.8)

For Susie, following the physical refers to her ghostly followings of the living, but also to her making love to Ray, using Ruth's body, a couple of chapters later. Susie needs that consensual sexual encounter to, in a sense, get back what Harvey tried to take from her. Likewise, Fenerman probably needs to remind himself that sex can be beautiful and good.

Ruth Connor Character Analysis

Ruth is Susie's age, fourteen, when Susie dies. She and Susie had recently become friends, connecting over Ruth's art. Ruth is ghost-Susie's Earthly counterpart. Susie wishes she were alive and is constantly pressing against the Inbetween, trying to break through to Earth. Ruth, would prefer to be on the other side of the divide and is pressing on the Inbetween from the opposite direction.

Ruth sees the dark side of Earthly life. She isn't suicidal, but she sees Earth as place with more bad than good. After Susie dies, she tells Ray, "Well, as my dad would say, it means she's out of this shithole" (6.119). Does Ruth change her opinion of Earth by the end of the novel? What do you think?

Ruth and Susie

Ruth and Susie were developing a friendship on Earth, but their relationship intensifies when Susie dies. Susie touches Ruth's shoulder when she's escaping Mr. Harvey to the afterlife. Ruth sees her, and it changes her life forever. She becomes obsessed with Susie and with women and girls who died of violent crimes. She also turns to vegetarianism, instantly drawing parallels between Susie's slaughter and the slaughter of animals. Her obsession with Susie transforms her art. Before Susie's death, she focused on drawing. Afterwards, however, she gets into poetry and journal writing.

Ruth becomes a memorialist, a chronicler of what's been hidden or forgotten. She sees New York City as a map of the dead – one which needs to be charted, recorded, and remembered. This devotion is what makes her a superstar in heaven, where the victims of the crimes Ruth discovers watch her like an afternoon soap. This is what makes her welcome in heaven. It gives her the unique privilege of going to heaven and giving talks before she dies. Her generosity in loaning Susie her body also rates big applause among the inhabitants of Susie's heaven.

Ruth and Alice Sebold

Ruth is also something of a ringer for her author. Like Alice Sebold, she dresses all in black, is pale, slender, and left her suburban home for New York City upon graduating high school. Like Sebold, Ruth is inspired to beautiful, terrible art by the very persuasive ghost of Susie Salmon. Like Sebold, Ruth feels like a total alien growing up in the suburbs, and like Sebold, she can't get away from it fast enough. Sebold writes,

Who would have thought that the place I most despised growing up - where I felt like the weirdest freak and the biggest loser - would turn out to be a gift to me. (source)

Like Ruth, Sebold must return, at least in imagination, and she must chronicle what she learns.

Ruth's Sexuality

"I'll make you a deal," Ruth said. "You can pretend I'm Susie and I will too ." (16.28)

Ruth is still in the process of forging a sexual identity. The unique bond between Ray, Susie, and Ruth make for an interesting love triangle. Ruth and Ray practice kiss, even though they claim not to be interested in each other romantically. Ray is still in love with Susie, and Ruth might or might not prefer women to men, or she might be bisexual. Susie and Ruth are little ambiguous on this point. Susie says,

It was not so much, she would write in her journals, that she wanted to have sex with women, but that she wanted to disappear inside them forever, to hide. (10.26)

We aren't exactly sure what Ruth is hiding from, other than the general horror or the world, or if she ever does have a sexual relationship with a woman. It's hinted that she and Ray continue their sexual relationship, or, perhaps, that both of them simply have their eyes open to the healing properties of sex, which Susie (and Marvin Gaye) are both so big on.

Ray Singh Character Analysis

Ray Singh is Susie's first crush, first kiss, and first love. He and Susie were just getting to know each other when she died. The love letter he slipped into her schoolbooks on the day of her death is only read by her from heaven. Seeing Susie taken from her life right at the moment she's embarking on her first romance makes her death seem all the more cruel. Susie doesn't dwell on Ray's process of grief, but it's obvious that this early tragic loss marks his life.

Other than his kissing experiments with Ruth, it doesn't seem that Ray had any romantic relationships after Susie's death. It looks like he was a virgin too when Susie borrows Ruth's body and makes love to him. Ray's romantic encounter with Susie/Ruth probably seems to have the effect of freeing all involved from being bound unhealthily together. Afterwards, Ruth and Ray can feel free to live again, and Susie to move on up to the wide wide Heaven.

Samuel Heckler Character Analysis

Samuel is Lindsey's boyfriend. About the time Susie leaves her life, Samuel enters it, bearing half-a-heart pendants, kisses, and unlimited moral support. Samuel is super smart and super athletic like Lindsey. In one of the novel's most romantic moments, when Samuel and Lindsey get engaged in the abandoned Victorian house, we learn that Samuel is important to the building motif we see throughout the novel. When he says he wants to renovate the Victorian house, Lindsey calls him "Samuel Heckler […] fixer of broken things" (17.48). He's integral to the Salmon family's rebuilding process; the life he builds with Lindsey includes a new baby, which Susie views as the ultimate symbol of rebuilding.

Grandma Lynn Character Analysis

Lynn is Abigail Salmon's mom. She's a hard drinking, hard flirting, fashion conscious lady who comes to the rescue after Susie's death, keeping Salmon house and just plain being there. Without Lynn things would have been much harder for the Salmons. She also earns endless brownie points from Susie for recognizing Harvey as her killer at Susie's funeral.

Abigail Suzanne Character Analysis

Abigail Suzanne is Lindsey and Samuel's baby, who we see for just a moment at the end of the novel. She is important to the idea of renewal and renovation in the novel.

Hal Heckler Character Analysis

Hal is Samuel's older brother. He rides a motorcycle and has a motorcycle repair shop across from the sinkhole where Susie's body is dumped. Although not a major character, he becomes very important to all the Salmons. Not only does he spend quality time with Buckley, and give Lindsey rides, but through his connection with the son of one of Harvey's first victims, Sophie Cichetti, he helps law enforcement connect some of the dots with regard to Mr. Harvey.

Mrs. Ruana Singh Character Analysis

Ruana is Ray's mom. She's a supportive figure, who eventually becomes friends with Jack and Abigail after Susie's death. Although not a major character, she does drive an important element of the plot. When Jack reveals his suspicions about Mr. Harvey, she tells him, "When I was sure [...] I would find a quiet way and I would kill him" (6.184). This advice is floating in Jack's ears when he almost baseball bats Clarissa, who he thinks is Harvey, in the cornfield that night. Oops!

Clarissa Character Analysis

Clarissa is Susie's close friend when she's alive. But, Clarissa can't hold up to the demands of being friends with a dead person. Granted, the scene with Jack Salmon sort of attacking her in the cornfield would alienate anybody, but she didn't have to go gossip about it at school. Sheesh! Susie definitely resents this and Clarissa's failure to remember her. This bitterness comes out in Susie's unromantic description of Clarissa's sex life.

Brian Nelson Character Analysis

Brian is Clarissa's boyfriend. He beats Jack in the knee with a baseball bat when Jack almost attacks Clarissa, thinking she's Mr. Harvey.

Holly Character Analysis

Holly is Susie's roommate in her first heaven, but we don't get her back-story. Since she's in Susie's heaven, and seems to relate to her situation, we assume she had a similar kind of death. Since there aren't a lot of subplots going on in Susie's heaven (the action all being down on Earth) Holly doesn't play a pivotal role in the novel.

Franny Character Analysis

Franny is Susie's "intake counselor" in the first heaven. As with Susie, her profession in life, counselor, continues into the afterlife. Franny, unlike Susie, knows the ways of the afterworld, and provides Susie with advice, support, lime cool-aid, and tells her how to get to a deeper realm of the heavenly afterworld. Like Holly she isn't involved in any plots or subplots.

Granddad Character Analysis

Granddad seems to be Jack's dad. Susie meets him in heaven and later goes to live with him in wide wide Heaven. They tour Earth together, and are both watching on the day that Mr. Harvey meets his death by icicle.

Sophie Cichetti Character Analysis

Sophie was a 49-year-old woman who rented Mr. Harvey a room and had sex with him consensually in 1960, after which he murdered her. Mr. Salmon remembers Harvey telling them that his late wife's name was Sophie. Creepy.

Ralph Cichetti Character Analysis

Ralph is Sophie's son. He's a Hell's Angel, who knows Hal Heckler through Hal's bike shop. Eventually, they realize that Susie and Sophie are victims of the same man.

Leida Johnson Character Analysis

Leida was six when Mr. Harvey murdered her in 1960. She's his youngest victim.

Flora Hernandez Character Analysis

Flora was eight years old when she was raped and murdered by Harvey in 1963.

Jackie Meyer Character Analysis

Jackie was thirteen when Mr. Harvey raped and murdered her in 1967.

Leah Fox Character Analysis

Leah was twelve when Mr. Harvey raped and murdered her in 1969. When Len Fenerman asks Mr. Harvey the name of his late wife, he tells him it's Leah.

Wendy Richter Character Analysis

Wendy was thirteen when Mr. Harvey raped and murdered her in 1971.

Unnamed Waitress Character Analysis

We are told that Mr. Harvey raped and murdered a waitress sometime after he murdered Susie.

Teenage Girl Character Analysis

At the end of the novel, we are shown a teenage girl who is almost Mr. Harvey's next victim. She walks away, but was probably only spared by the falling icicle which sends Mr. Harvey to his snowy grave.

Clair Character Analysis

Clair is a New Jersey girl Mr. Harvey managed to entice into his van. Luckily, she got away unharmed.

Holiday Character Analysis

Holiday is the Salmon family's beloved pooch. When he dies, he goes to Susie's heaven.

Nate Character Analysis

Nate is Buckley's friend. Buckley stays at Nate's house when Susie is initially missing. Nate is the person Buckley tells that he can see Susie after she is dead.

Mr. Connor Character Analysis

Mr. Connor is Ruth's dad. Although not a major figure, he contributes to the building motif. Near the end of the story, Samuel learns that the old Victorian house he and Lindsey found is owned

by Mr. Connor. Conner has just opened a renovation company, and he hires Samuel to work for him.

Mr. Peterford and Miss Ryan Character Analysis

These are teachers at Susie's junior high. They give Ruth a hard time because she draws anatomically correct nude women in art class.

Mrs. Dewitt Character Analysis

Mrs. Dewitt is Susie, Ray, and Ruth's English teacher.

Mr. Dewitt Character Analysis

Mr. Dewitt coaches the boys' soccer team, which Lindsey is allowed to try out for.

Mr. Botte Character Analysis

Mr. Botte is Susie's biology teacher, her favorite teacher. About eighteen months after Susie dies, he loses his daughter to leukemia.

Mrs. Stead Character Analysis

Mrs. Stead is a therapist at Susie's school. She tells Len Fenerman that Susie was reading *Othello* and *To Kill A Mockingbird*.

Principle Caden Character Analysis

Principal Caden is the principal at Susie's school. He tries but fails to comfort Lindsey after Susie's death.

Mrs. Koekle Character Analysis

Mrs. Koekle is Buckley's kindergarten teacher, on whom he has a crush.

The Utemeyers Character Analysis

Bethel Utemeyer is the oldest inhabitant of Susie's heaven. Susie had attended her funeral. Apparently, she lost her daughter, Natalie, when Natalie was a child. Natalie and her mother are reunited in Susie's heaven.

Reverend Strick Character Analysis

The reverend that presides over Susie's funeral.

Artie Character Analysis

Artie is the son of a mortician. He's known for chasing people with imaginary syringes filled with imaginary embalming fluid. The boy also draws these things all over his notebooks. At the Gifted and Talented Symposium, he turns out to be an OK guy, and he tries to be a friend to Lindsey.

Joe Ellis Character Analysis

Joe Ellis is at first the scapegoat for Mr. Harvey's crimes against neighborhood pets. He never gets over being accused of hurting animals.

Grace Tarking Character Analysis

Grace is Susie's neighbor, a girl around her age. She is Susie's first photography subject, when Susie gets her first camera.

Literary Devices

Symbols, Imagery, Allegory

Susie's Jingly Cap

The only sound I made after that was a weak tinkling of bells. (1.81)

Susie's jingly cap is a homemade symbol of her mother's love and care. Harvey perverts it, using it to gag Susie while he rapes her. It becomes a symbol of her loss of breath and voice. When Len Fenerman recovers her hat and shows it to Abigail and Jack, it becomes a symbol that great harm has come to Susie. The hat though, also leads us back to the roots of the American horror story – yes, back to Edgar Allan Poe.

In Poe's " The Cask of Amontillado," a tale of revenge and murder, the narrator murders Fortunato (dressed like a jester, complete with jingly cap) by walling him up in a tiny underground space. Before the narrator puts in the last brick of the wall he's enclosing Fortunato in, he makes sure that Fortunato, like Susie, no longer has voice to protest. He says that, at the end, "There came forth in return only a jingling of the bells." We also think of bells as

tolling for the dead. In the case of both Susie and the ironically named Fortunato, the jingling of bells are one of the last sounds they hear.

The Red Scarf
"Why do you have my mother's scarf?" (16: Snapshots.36)

The bright red scarf Lindsey sees on Len Fenerman's desk clearly belongs to her mother. When Lindsey sees it, and asks Len about it, she realizes the truth of the affair. Now, we notice that Shakespeare's tragic *Othello* is referenced quite a few times in the novel. A similar handkerchief is a huge symbol in that play.

Here's a crash course in *Othello*: The handkerchief, Othello's first gift to his wife Desdemona, is a symbol of her fidelity so long as it's in her possession, but a symbol of her supposed infidelity when the evil Iago plants it on Cassio. The catch is, Desdemona isn't unfaithful. So, the handkerchief becomes a symbol of the type of jealousy that leads Othello to murder his wife.

Although Lindsey and Buckley become jealous of Abigail's life outside of them, jealousy isn't a quality exhibited by Jack, and he never learns of the affair. So, the scarf is transformed in this novel. It becomes a symbol of the fact that Abigail made her own choices about whom to have sex with, and isn't required to die as a result. This is also a sharp contrast to the fate of her daughter, who didn't have a choice and who, in some ways, dies because of Mr. Harvey's jealousy and desire to destroy her and the perfect world he can never share.

The Monopoly Shoe
[Buckley to Jack:] "I saved the Monopoly shoe and then it was gone. You took it. You act like she was only yours!" (18.60)

Buckley is about four when Susie dies, and, while he never completely understands what happened to her, he has a fair idea. When it seems clear to the family that she's met a bad end, Jack tries to explain the absence of the beloved sister to Buckley over a game of Monopoly. The Monopoly shoe was always Susie's piece. The removal of her piece from the game is what Jack uses to illustrate to Buckley her removal from the game of life, and he gives it to Buckley as a memento of his sister.

But, when it turns up missing it becomes, for Buckley, a symbol of what Susie's death has taken from him – namely, his father's love and attention throughout the years. In the difficult moment, Buckley begs him to let go of the dead and be there for him, the living. The very idea of stopping his continued vigil for Susie is so threatening to Jack that he has a heart attack.

The Broken Heart Necklace
Days after Susie's murder, Samuel Heckler enters Lindsey's life in earnest. He gives her half a golden heart, and wears the other half on a cord around his neck. This seems like a nod to David Lynch's *Twin Peaks*, another story of murder in a 'perfect' neighborhood, by an insider.

Fans will remember that James gives Laura Palmer just such a broken heart necklace, which really is a symbol of broken love.

In *The Lovely Bones* it's a symbol that Lindsey and Samuel are joined at the heart, but also of the hearts are broken by Susie's death. Samuel's gift shows Lindsey that while he wants her love, he knows her heart is broken, and he wants to help heal it. And, it's true, he proves utterly devoted to Lindsey, and their romance is a sweet balm against the many gruesome aspects of the novel.

Setting

Mostly Suburban Pennsylvania and the Afterlife, 1973 - 1984

The Lovely Bones is set mostly in an unnamed Pennsylvania suburb (called Norristown in the film version). Alice Sebold grew up in the suburbs, which she refers to as "Nowhere USA" and draws from the experience for this novel. She says, "Who would have thought that the place I most despised growing up – where I felt like the weirdest freak and the biggest loser – would turn out to be a gift to me" (source).

The novel also follows Ruth Connors to New York City, Mr. Harvey to Connecticut and Maine, and Abigail Salmon to California. If that's not exciting enough, it features glimpses of two different heavens Susie inhabits. From these places, she observes the Earthly goings-on she describes to us.

The Lovely Bones begins on December 6, 1973, with Susie's brutal beating, rape, murder, and dismemberment by her neighbor Mr. Harvey. This is back before we knew that serial killers were commonly known about. Like Susie says, "It was still back when people believed things like that didn't happen" (1.1). This collective innocence (which the digital/informational/technological age would soon rectify) is part of why Susie consents to enter Mr. Harvey's underground trap. It's also why Detective Len Fenerman doesn't figure Harvey for a killer.

Then novel ends in the spring or summer of 1984 and weaves backwards and forwards through time from the date of Susie's death. Susie remembers her earlier life. She also learns about Mr. Harvey's, while watching the lives of those she left behind over the next ten years.

The Salmon House and The Harvey House

Mr. Harvey has positioned himself in the eye of temptation: a suburban family neighborhood, with a house overlooking the schools, the soccer field, and the cornfield. His normal-looking suburban house is a big part of his disguise of innocence, and it allows him to blend unnoticed into suburbia.

Since it's part of the same planned development, Harvey's house has the exact same floor plan as the Salmons'. In dreadful irony, Susie and Harvey occupied the same bedroom in their respective homes. While the two houses might be identical in design, the designs of their respective inhabitants are totally opposite. So, Harvey's house is like the evil twin to the Salmons'.

The issue of the repeating floor plans in suburban developments is compelling to Sebold. She says,

[…] I [was] made aware […] that while I grew up hearing that there were 'a thousand stories in the naked city and none of them the same' this was as true of the look-alike houses all around me as it was of the places I lived as an adult. The difference perhaps is that you have to look harder in the suburbs, past the floor plans and into the human heart. (source).

Susie and Lindsey find the parallels between their house and Mr. Harvey's quite compelling as well. In the climactic scene where Lindsey daringly (and dangerously!) infiltrates Harvey's house, Lindsey goes into memory overload imagining the scenes that happened in her home before Susie's death. For Susie, this infiltration of her killer's home by her sister opens up information she's been seeking, the details of Harvey's hideous work. She tells us,

The architecture of my murderer's life , the bodies of the girls he'd left behind, began to reveal itself to me now that my sister was in that house. I stood in heaven. I called their names […] (14.31).

Susie sees the elements of the world, people, things, events, as parts (or bones) of structures always in the process of being built. The dead girls are the bones of Mr. Harvey and Susie's tragically interconnected stories.

The Afterworld
Susie presents us with an intriguing vision of the afterlife. Compared with life on Earth, the afterlife offers Susie much more control over her environment. She can have it her way, with two conditions: 1) no way to go back to life on Earth, and 2) limited ability to communicate with the living. But, she can do all the Earth-watching she wants. Susie also describes two types of heavens: heaven and wide wide Heaven.

heaven: Susie's a junior high school girl who's just suffered a horrific trauma and was wrenched away from her life without any preparation. Her first heaven has a counselor (Franny), other murdered girls, kids playing sports, high schools without teachers, frolicking puppies, junk food, and fashion magazines. Like Susie says, "We had been given, in our heavens, our simplest dreams" (2.17).

Luckily, she isn't stuck with the desires she comes to heaven with. She grows and changes, and her heaven adapts. Franny (in a *Field of Dreams* moment) explains, "All you have to do is

desire it, and if you desire it enough and understand why [...] it will come" (2.25).

wide wide Heaven: Susie's knowledge of the cosmic design continues to grow throughout the story. She learns that if she stops worrying about her family, about why Harvey killed her, and about stopping him from killing others she can go to a different kind of heaven.

Eventually, Susie makes a transition to "wide wide Heaven" (Epilogue.15). This heaven seems to be a place where imagination, chilling out, and having fun are perfected. Susie says,

It's about flathead nails and the soft down of new leaves and wild roller coaster rides and escaped marbles that fall then hang then take you somewhere you could never have imagined in your small heaven dreams. (Epilogue.16)

Even this heaven seems desire-based, and Susie never makes the claim that everybody goes to it. According to her cosmology, your heaven might also match your religious beliefs. Hers includes Evensong, Anglican evening prayer, and the people around her share her wish to perform it.

Harvey in h/Heaven? Susie never discusses what happens to Mr. Harvey when he dies. She can see everybody on Earth, but she can't see them in the afterworld unless they are with her in her heaven. What do you think? Will Harvey go to a place where his desires are fulfilled, like Susie's are? And what are his desires? Will he still want to rape and kill, or does he have deeper desires, like having love, a family, *not* wanting to hurt others? Will he desire punishment for his crimes on Earth? Should he receive punishment for his crimes on Earth?

In John Milton's *Paradise Lost* Satan says, "The mind is its own place, and in it self/ Can make a Heav'n of Hell, a Hell of Heav'n" (line 255). Should/could Mr. Harvey escape the hell of the mind in the afterlife? Should we be taking advice from Satan?

The Inbetween
Hours before I died, my mother hung on the refrigerator a picture that Buckley had drawn. In the drawing a thick blue line separated the air from the ground. [...] I became convinced that the thick blue line was a real place, where Heaven's horizon met Earth's . (3.175)

The Inbetween seems to be the border between the afterworld and Earth, as depicted by Buckley in his prescient drawing. It takes great effort on Susie's part to pass from the afterworld through the Inbetween, to the Earth, though it's easy to pass back. Sometimes (like when she's riding trains) it's not entirely clear whether Susie is just watching or actually absent from the afterworld and present on Earth in ghostly essence. There's some indication that she's simply gotten better at passing through the Inbetween to Earth.

In Peter Jackson's film adaptation, The Inbetween is the name of the heaven Susie goes to when she first dies. Critics haven't been all that enthusiastic about the film. They claim that

Jackson's the Inbetween is too darn fluffy and pretty. Since Shmoop is a pillar of neutrality on such issues, we leave it to you to decide.

The Sinkhole

The sinkhole is where Mr. Harvey dumps Susie's body parts, locked inside a heavy safe. (Ironic use of a safe, isn't it?) When Ray, Ruth, and Harvey all converge there for a moment in 1982, Susie gets really excited. So excited, she manages to borrow Ruth's body so she can make love to Ray in Hal Heckler's nearby bike shop.

According to Susie's dad, the sinkhole (an opening in the earth) is a result of the collapse of an underground mine. The sinkhole constantly swallows and regurgitates the stuff that's been dumped in it. When the players converge in that area, the sinkhole is about to be covered over, and Susie's body along with it. No wonder Susie gets so excited.

The sinkhole also seems kind of analogous to Mr. Harvey. The sinkhole is a rupture in the earth, which can be dangerous, swallow things up and hold them underground. Harvey ruptures families, swallowing up their girls and holding them underground. Like the sinkhole, even when wearing a disguise of stability, Harvey is still dangerous.

Crime Scenes

From the Stolfutz Cornfield where Susie was murdered to the shack in the woods in Connecticut where Mr. Harvey murders and buries a waitress, *The Lovely Bones* is loaded with crime scenes. Most of them are discovered psychically by Ruth in New York City and duly recorded in her journal. This gives her great standing with the murdered woman and girls in heaven, who want badly to see their deaths recognized by the living. Like Susie (before she matures) they are needy and want to be remembered and talked about.

The way the world looks to Ruth is similar to the way it looks to Len Fenerman – full of crime scenes. But there are some differences. From Len's point of view, it's all about preserving order in society. The crime scenes are disruptions in the society. For Ruth, these disruptions dominate the landscape. She's about preserving the scenes in memory, through writing and art, and about pleasing the girls in heaven with these memorial activities.

The Victorian House and the Salmon House

Usually if you see an old abandoned house…in the rain…in a horror story, you should know better than to go into it! We're talking to you Lindsey and Samuel. Luckily, their horror story is kind of ending at this point, so it's safe for them to go inside. And it's a good thing they do, because the abandoned Victorian house proves a romantic counterpoint to all the novel's gruesome and seriously supernatural settings. In this house, Lindsey and Samuel get engaged and even stop lightning and thunder when they are about to make love.

By running home eight miles in the rain in their skivvies to keep Mr. Salmon from worrying about them, they help bring happiness and new life back into the Salmon house. Lindsey and Samuel

getting married and staying in town to raise their child helps the Salmon house become a home again. Samuel and Lindsey's subsequent restoration of the old Victorian house keeps with the building/rebuilding motif running through the novel, and with its ultimate insistence on hope for renewal and after tragedy.

What's Up With the Title?

The title is oh-so-creepily inviting. It combines, in the spirit of horror and Gothic conventions – love, life, death, and beauty. It also provides us with suspense and mystery – we want to know whose bones these, are and why they might be seen as lovely.

Mr. Harvey

Let's try out Mr. Harvey's perspective. He doesn't keep the bones of his human victims (though he'd probably like too). Nope, his bone collection comes from the neighborhood pets, whose disappearances are at first blamed on the unfortunate Joe Ellis. Susie tells us, "What I think was hardest for me to realize was that he had tried each time to stop himself. He had killed animals, lesser lives, to keep from killing a child" (11.21). Fans of *Twilight* and Anne Rice's vampire tales will recognize that tune. In any case, the animal bones are (possibly) lovely because they represent moments when Harvey resists his desires to rape, brutalize, and murder people.

Susie's Loved Ones

At first, all we can think about is the elbow – the only bone of Susie's that is found. It gives the people who love her proof positive that something horrible has happened to her, but it also gives them hope at first. If the other bones aren't found, it's possible that Susie might still be alive even though she might not have an arm anymore. Of course, this hope is bitterly dashed. Her bones are lovely to her loved ones not in hope, but in their memories of her.

Susie

Late in the novel, when her family is celebrating together, Susie reveals what the title means to her:

These were the lovely bones that had grown around my absence [...]. And I began to see things in a way that let me hold the world without me in it. (23.97)

This is some pretty abstract talk, what we might expect from a ghost, but we can follow. Susie is saying that a) she sees her loved ones and their stories as the bones of a body of earthly happiness, of life; and b) she can stop anxiously hovering over them, because they are OK.

But, the sentence that follows the above complicates matters. Susie says,

The events that my death wrought were merely the bones of a body that would become whole at some unpredictable time in the future. (23.97)

We've thought about this a lot, even had a few meetings about it, and have come to the conclusion that Susie is waiting for the day when her loved ones are all dead with her; then the "body" will be "whole." Sounds morbid, but that's natural for the dead. We think it's a good thing. In Susie's expanding understanding of the world, human life is really short and is followed by a seemingly eternal afterlife. So, death is no longer something to be feared; it's the bulk of existence.

Yet, no amount of philosophical high-roading can stop Susie from wanting herself and her loved ones in the same place. Hence, her wishes for their deaths, as well as for their happy lives. She knows she can't go back to them, so they have to come to her.

What's Up With the Ending?

I could not have what I wanted most. Mr. Harvey dead and me living. Heaven wasn't perfect .
(2.39)

The ending is about as happy as a book about a murdered girl can get. It features the fulfillment of one of Susie's utmost desires, articulated in Chapter 2 (and in the quote up top). Mr. Harvey is interrupted from pursuing his latest teen victim, and plummeted to his death by, of all things, a falling icicle. Said icicle might or might not have been dislodged by Susie's ghostly interference. We like to think she had a hand in things. Notice also that Harvey's death by icicle is cleverly foreshadowed at a midpoint in the novel. Susie tells us:

In heaven, "How to Commit the Perfect Murder" was an old game. I always chose the icicle: the weapon melts away. (10.139)

Ahh yes, revenge is sweet, but Susie's desire for Mr. Harvey's death is based more in preventing him from hurting others than revenge for its own sake. Even though she's already in "wide wide Heaven" (see "Setting" for more), she can only truly stop her Earth-angst if she doesn't have to worry about this creep hurting people. Mr. Harvey's death begs a question: Where does he go when he dies? What do you think?

Creepy ponderings aside, that tragically happy aspect of the ending is followed by the next best thing to the restoration of Susie's life on Earth: the birth of her niece and namesake, baby Abigail Suzanne, the baby of super-couple Lindsey and Samuel. The birth gives the novel a sense of formal unity. A novel that begins with the death of a young girl, ends with the birth of another. She won't replace Susie, of course, but she can help Susie's loved ones heal.

Did You Know?

Trivia

- When asked about her writing process, Sebold said, "I don't outline and plan, I just work with what I unattractively call 'the subconscious stew.'" Of her daily writing habits she says, "I wake up very early in the morning. I like to start in the dark, and I never work at night, because my brain is evaporated by 4 p.m." (source)

- Alice Sebold says: "whereas in *Lovely Bones* the rape and murder scene was the first thing I wrote, in *Lucky* [Sebold's nonfiction account of being raped and the aftermath] it was the last; the first chapter in *Lucky* is the last part I wrote." (source)

- Sebold's debut book, *Lucky* (1999) is a well received piece of nonfiction about Sebold's rape and the aftermath, including Sebold testifying against her rapist in court, and sending him to prison. You can read a little of *Lucky* on Google Books.

- Dead narrators, like Susie, are become a popular conceit, especially in novel's featuring young adults. (source)

Steaminess Rating

R
The R rating is earned at the beginning of the novel, where narrator Susie Salmon recounts, from her heavenly post, the details of her rape and murder. There are also details of her killer's previous violent crimes. There are also plenty of loving, consensual sexual moments (none very graphically described) to counterpoint the sexual brutality. *The Lovely Bones* always depicts healthy, consensual sex as a positive healing activity.

Allusions and Cultural References

Literary and Philosophical References

- Juan Ramón Jiménez Mantecón (1.2)
- Victor Hugo, *The Hunchback of Notre Dame* (1.37)
- Harper Lee, *To Kill A Mockingbird* (2.85, 2.93)
- William Shakespeare, *Othello* *(2.90, 2.91, 2.92, 6.28)*
- Erica Jong, *Fear of Flying* (2.155)
- Judy Blume, *Are You There God, It's Me Margaret* (2.158)
- Albert Camus, *Resistance, Rebellion, and Death* (2.158)
- Thornton Wilder, *Our Town* (3.34)
- William Shakespeare (6.26)
- John Howard Griffin, *Black Like Me* (6.29)
- Roald Dahl, *James and the Giant Peach* (7.36)
- Henry James (12.104)
- T.S. Eliot (12.104)
- Charles Dickens (12.104)
- *Norton Anthology* (13.171)
- Sylvia Plath, *The Bell Jar* (16.15)
- Moliere (16.69)
- Jean-Paul Sartre (16.69)
- Collette (16.69)
- Marcel Proust (16.69)
- Gustave Flaubert (16.69)

Historical References

- Royal Shakespeare Company (6.26)
- Margaret Sanger (12.95)
- Gloria Steinem (12.95)
- *Gray's Anatomy* (16: Snapshots.33) (the book)

Mythic References

- Persephone (12.88, 12.102)
- Zeus (12.88)
- Helen of Troy (12.95)
- Demeter (12.102)
- Cupid (12.102
- Psyche (12.102)

Pop Culture References

- *Breakfast at Tiffany's* (2.7) (the movie)
- *Seventeen* (2.17)
- *Glamour* (2.17)
- *Vogue* (2.17)
- Barbie (2.99)
- Raggedy Ann (2.99)
- The Marx Brothers (2.156)
- Kool-Aid (2.20)
- Charles Bronson (5.1)
- Monopoly (5.86)
- Strawberry Banana Kissing Potion (6.33)
- Sir Laurence Olivier (6.37)
- *Playboy* (11.110)
- Dr. Spock (12.104)
- *Better Homes and Gardens Guide to Entertaining* (12.104)
- *Masterpiece Theatre* (18.21)

Best of the Web

Websites

Sebold's Current Webpage
http://www.hachettebookgroup.com/features/alicesebold/index.html#utm_source=alicesebold.com&utm_medium=redirect&utm_campaign=print
This focuses on her latest book, *The Almost Moon.*

Sebold's Page at Hachette Books
http://www.hachettebookgroup.com/authors_Alice-Sebold-%281003757%29.htm
Be sure and click on the links to two essays written by Sebold.

The Website for the Film
http://www.lovelybones.com/alice-sebold.html#home
The music is slightly sappy, but this is still a neat website.

Alice Sebold's Facebook Page
http://www.facebook.com/pages/Alice-Sebold/24541550878

You know you want to friend her!

Serial Murder
http://www.fbi.gov/page2/july08/serialmurder_070708.html
Read what the FBI has to say about serial killers.

Movie or TV Productions
The 2009 Film Adaptation
http://www.imdb.com/title/tt0380510/
Directed by Peter Jackson, of *Lord of the Rings* fame.

Documents
An Interview
http://www.powells.com/authors/sebold.html
Alice Sebold discusses writing *Lucky* and *The Lovely Bones*.

A Review
http://www.powells.com/review/2002_08_12.html
This is, like most, a positive review. It's from *The Christian Science Monitor.*

Another Review
http://dir.salon.com/books/review/2002/08/01/sebold/
This one is from *Salon's* Laura Miller.

Movie Review
http://www.telegraph.co.uk/culture/film/filmreviews/7257319/The-Lovely-Bones-review.html
This review from the *Telegraph* is like most of the film's reviews – thumbs down. This article calls the movie "a turkey, a pig's ear, a mad cow of a film."

Another Review of the Film
http://www.cnn.com/2009/SHOWBIZ/Movies/12/11/lovely.bones/index.html
This one is from *EW*. They're not really fans either.

"A Day Out With Saoirse Ronan and Rose McIver"
http://www.nytimes.com/2010/01/17/fashion/17night.html
Meet the girls who play Susie and Lindsey in the movie.

"Shockwaves"
http://www.lovelybones.com/alice-sebold.html#home
A article from *People* about Sebold and *The Lovely Bones.*

Video

"A Key Moment Reimagined"
http://www.etonline.com/news/2010/04/86003/
A brief article featuring a clip from the film.

A Video Interview
http://www.collider.com/2010/01/12/stanley-tucci-video-interview-the-lovely-bones/
See what Stanley Tucci, who plays Mr. Harvey in the movie, has to say about his role.

The Hollywood Premier of the Film
http://www.youtube.com/watch?v=U1R9Uz7G_80
Be there with the stars!

An Interview
http://www.youtube.com/watch?v=VYXpMpFoq04
Saoirse Ronan (Susie) and Rose McIver (Lindsey) give an interview.

Audio

Samuel Barber's "Adagio for Strings"
http://www.youtube.com/watch?v=RRMz8fKkG2g
Susie and her grandfather dance to this song in heaven.

Images

The Author
http://www.popculturemadness.com/Entertainment/Books/images/AliceSebold.jpg
Here Alice Sebold looks infinitely wise.

A Book Cover
http://image3.examiner.com/images/blog/EXID19494/images/resized_the_lovely_bones.jpg
This cover is far less creepy than the one that came out with the movie.

A Book Cover
http://www.inthestacks.tv/wp-content/uploads/2010/02/TheLovelyBonesCover.jpg
And here's the book cover that came out with the movie.